the RETURN OF the king
study guide

By michael poteet

D1470363

Progeny Press

Limited permission to reproduce this study guide.

Purchase of this study guide entitles an individual teacher
to reproduce pages for use in the classroom or home.
Multiple teachers may not reproduce pages
from the same study guide.

The Return of the King Study Guide
A Progeny Press Study Guide
by Michael Poteet
edited by Michael S. Gilleland
cover artwork by Mary R. Gilleland
cover design and color by Nathan Gilleland

Printed in the United States of America.

ISBN: 978-1-58609-372-3 Book
        978-1-58609-619-9 CD
        978-1-58609-464-5 Set

Study Guide Author

The Rev. Michael S. Poteet is an ordained minister in the Presbyterian Church (USA), currently pastoring a congregation in Clifton Heights, Pennsylvania. A native Texan, Mr. Poteet earned an undergraduate degree in English and Religion at the College of William and Mary in Virginia and earned his Masters of Divinity degree at Princeton Theological Seminary. In addition to writing for Progeny Press, Mr. Poteet has published short fiction in *Star Trek: Strange New Worlds II* (Pocket Books, 1999) and *Leaps of Faith: An Anthology of Christian Science Fiction* (FrancisIsidore Electronic Press, 2003). Mr. Poteet also writes regularly for LinC, a youth resource for the United Methodist Church. He is married with one child.

Peer Review Panel

The Rev. Michael S. Poteet is an ordained minister in the Presbyterian Church (USA), currently pastoring a congregation in Clifton Heights, Pennsylvania. A native Texan, Mr. Poteet earned an undergraduate degree in English and Religion at the College of William and Mary in Virginia and earned his Masters of Divinity degree at Princeton Theological Seminary. In addition to writing for Progeny Press, Mr. Poteet has published short fiction in *Star Trek: Strange New Worlds II* (Pocket Books, 1999) and *Leaps of Faith: An Anthology of Christian Science Fiction* (FrancisIsidore Electronic Press, 2003). Mr. Poteet also writes regularly for LinC, a youth resource for the United Methodist Church. He is married with one child.

Calvin Roso is a full-time instructor at Oral Roberts University and consults Christian schools in the area of curriculum design and evaluation. He has taught high school English for nine years and teaches workshops in the United States and Latin America on the topics of literature and curriculum. In addition to writing several study guides, Mr. Roso has published a number of articles on curriculum for Christian schools. He earned his Bachelor's Degree in English Education from the University of Wisconsin—Madison and a Master's Degree in Education from Oral Roberts University, where he is currently pursuing a Doctorate in Education.

Janice DeLong is Associate Professor of Education at Liberty University in Lynchburg, Virginia where she teaches children's literature and supervises student teachers. Prior to coming to Liberty, she served on faculties in both public and private schools and has experience in homeschooling, as well. Her husband, Robert, teaches psychology at Liberty. They are parents of four children. Mrs. DeLong is co-author of three books: *Core Collection for Small Libraries, Contemporary Christian Authors,* and *Young Adult Poetry: A Survey and Theme Guide.*

Peer Review Panel membership as of August 2003.

Table of Contents

Note to Instructor

How to Use Progeny Press Study Guides. Progeny Press study guides are designed to help students better understand and enjoy literature by getting them to notice and understand how authors craft their stories and to show them how to think through the themes and ideas introduced in the stories. To properly work through a Progeny Press study guide, students should have easy access to a good dictionary, a thesaurus, a Bible (we use NIV translation, but that is up to your preference; just be aware of some differences in language), and sometimes a topical Bible or concordance. Supervised access to the Internet also can be helpful at times, as can a good set of encyclopedias.

Most middle grades and high school study guides take from eight to ten weeks to complete, generally working on one section per week. Over the years, we have found that it works best if the students completely read the novel the first week, while also working on a prereading activity chosen by the parent or teacher. Starting the second week, most parents and teachers have found it works best to work on one study guide page per day until the chapter sections are completed. Students should be allowed to complete questions by referring to the book; many questions require some cross-reference between elements of the stories.

Most study guides contain an Overview section that can be used as a final test, or it can be completed in the same way the chapter sections were completed. If you wish to perform a final test but your particular study guide does not have an Overview section, we suggest picking a couple of questions from each section of the study guide and using them as your final test.

Most study guides also have a final section of essays and postreading activities. These may be assigned at the parents' or teachers' discretion, but we suggest that students engage in several writing or other extra activities during the study of the novel to complement their reading and strengthen their writing skills.

As for high school credits, most Christian high schools with whom we have spoken have assigned a value of one-fourth credit to each study guide, and this also seems to be acceptable to colleges assessing homeschool transcripts.

Internet References

All websites listed in this study guide were checked for appropriateness at the time of publication. However, due to the changing nature of the Internet, we cannot guarantee that the URLs listed will remain appropriate or viable. Therefore, we urge parents and teachers to take care in and exercise careful oversight of their children's use of the Internet.

Special Note to *The Lord of the Rings*

J. R. R. Tolkien essentially wrote *The Lord of the Rings* as one book, which was then divided by the publisher into *The Fellowship of the Ring, The Two Towers,* and *The Return of the King.* Though each book can be read on its own, to fully understand the themes and philosophy of the book, the full trilogy should be read. Progeny Press has produced study guides for all three novels of *The Lord of the Rings.*

    The Lord of the Rings has been named by some authorities as the greatest work of fiction of the 20th Century. The trilogy has captured readers' imaginations perhaps more than any other fiction of recent decades and has accumulated many devoted fans. Tolkien took great care in his creation of an alternate world, peopling it with an amazing variety of creatures, each with a fully developed history and language. The most avid fans of *The Lord of the Rings* have become expert in its languages and geography, in its history and mythology, and in the history and methods of its authorship.

    We will not attempt to delve into such matters in these study guides—others more expert than we have written numerous books and articles on the subjects. If the student wishes to pursue such interests he or she will find a list of resources at the end of this study guide in which he may begin his exploration.

    Tolkien also introduces many characters and themes in *The Fellowship of the Ring* and *The Two Towers* that he develops later in *The Return of the King.* Therefore, it can be difficult to fully trace or analyze themes unless the reader is familiar with all of the books. Because of this, we suggest that students at least *read* the entire trilogy, even if they do not study it. The themes Tolkien plants and nurtures in earlier parts of the story are not brought to fruition until the last book, and what may appear to be death or defeat in one book may be revealed as life and victory in the next.

    J. R. R. Tolkien was a devoted Christian, and the underlying assumptions and overlying themes in *The Lord of the Rings* are, in essence, Christian. Concerning wizards and magic in *The Lord of the Rings,* what may be called "magic" is used by both good and evil, but it is not a series of "spells" and incantations such as seen in popular fiction. In fact, some of the people of the story object to the word *magic,* and they object to their powers apparently being put in the same category as the evil powers. The "magic" in *The Lord of the Rings* derives from essential spiritual power in the same way that angels and demons have and use power. It should also be noted that while such power is used in *The Lord of the Rings,* it is not the main element—the story is truly about personal faith, struggle, and perseverance.

Synopsis

The Return of the King—the third volume (Books V and VI) of *The Lord of the Rings*—continues and concludes the story begun in *The Fellowship of the Ring* and *The Two Towers*.

Book Five begins with the members of the Fellowship dispersing again as they prepare to withstand the impending onslaught from the Dark Lord Sauron and his Nazgûl. Pippin and Gandalf arrive at the city of Minas Tirith, where the Men of Gondor will soon make a stand against the armies of Sauron. Denethor, Steward of Gondor, strives with Gandalf for power and supremacy as they prepare for Sauron's assault, but his pride comes crashing down as personal tragedy strikes and defeat looms.

Merry pledges himself to the service of the king of Rohan and, unwilling to stay behind as the king marches to the aid of Minas Tirith, he seeks a way to join the Riders of Rohan as they go to war. Gimli and Legolas follow Aragorn into the Paths of the Dead, from which no man has ever returned, in a desperate attempt to bring aid to Gondor before it is too late.

Eventually, the survivors of the assault on Gondor gather before the gates of Mordor in a desperate, hopeless attempt to engage Sauron again in battle and keep him distracted from the two lonely hobbits they believe are still alive, trying to find their way through the wastelands of Mordor to the seat of Sauron's power. Frodo and Sam must destroy the One Ring by casting it into the fires in which it was forged in the heart of Mount Doom. But at the crucial moment Frodo's strength finally fails.

The Return of the King brings to conclusion J. R. R. Tolkien's epic masterpiece of good versus evil, personal struggle, and redemption.

About the Novel's Author

John Ronald Reuel Tolkien was born on January 3, 1892, in Bloemfontein, South Africa, which was at this time under British rule. Tolkien's father, Arthur, managed a bank there. The hot climate made young Tolkien ill, however, and he, his brother Hilary, and their mother Mabel moved to Birmingham, England. Arthur intended to join his family, but was detained by business concerns and poor health. He died in 1896.

Tolkien now saw for the first time the English countryside, and he quickly fell in love with it. His mother's family came from Worcestershire County; that area would later appear in Middle-earth as The Shire, home of hobbits.[1]

Tolkien also grew to love foreign languages. His mother taught him Latin at home; he also found beauty in Welsh. His passion for linguistics would last his whole life, leading him both to his career as a philologist—a student of the structure of languages—and to his delight in inventing languages of his own. These private languages became the foundation for his elaborate Middle-earth mythology: "The 'stories' were made . . . to provide a world for the languages . . . . To me a name comes first and the story follows."[2]

Mabel not only taught her sons academic subjects but also nurtured them in their Christian faith. She left the Church of England to join the Roman Catholic Church. Both her sons served as altar boys at Birmingham Oratory, the church that virtually became their home when Mabel died in 1904. About her, Tolkien wrote:

> My own dear mother was a martyr indeed, and it is not to everybody that God grants so easy a way to his great gifts as he did to Hilary and myself, giving us a mother who killed herself with labour and trouble to ensure us keeping the faith.[3]

In 1908, Tolkien discovered another kind of love when he met Edith Bratt, a teenage orphan like himself. They married in 1916 and eventually had three sons. While Edith seems never to have fully appreciated Middle-earth, and while Tolkien's devotion to his mythology at times caused stress in the marriage, the relationship generally remained a happy one until Edith's death in 1971.

Having won a scholarship to Oxford University, Tolkien entered Exeter College in the fall of 1911, where he studied both Classics and English Language and Literature. After graduation, he was summoned for army service during World War I. In July 1916, his battalion fought in Ovillers, France, trying to free that village from German control. The effort failed; many of Tolkien's fellow soldiers and personal friends were killed. Tolkien would forever recall the "animal horror" of war.[4] The experience reveals itself in the imagined battles in the pages of *The Lord of the Rings*—and Tolkien used his mythological characters and concepts to express his feelings on real warfare. Writing to his son Christopher, who served in the Royal Air Force during World War II, Tolkien reflects that war is an "ultimately evil job. For we are attempting to conquer Sauron with the Ring. And we shall (it seems) succeed. But the penalty is, as you know, to breed new Saurons. . . ."[5]

In 1920, Tolkien became an instructor in English Language at the University of Leeds, and in 1925 he returned to Oxford to assume the Professorship of Anglo-Saxon. The publication of *The Hobbit* in 1937 brought him unexpected fame.

Although *The Hobbit* began as a story told to entertain Tolkien's young sons, the finished novel found wide approval with children and adults alike. The first edition sold out by Christmas. Tolkien's publisher wrote to him, "A large public will be clamouring next year to hear more from you about Hobbits!"[6] Dutifully, Tolkien attempted to write a further adventure for Bilbo Baggins—but instead of a sequel, Tolkien produced his epic novel, *The Lord of the Rings* (published, to Tolkien's regret, in three volumes: *The Fellowship of the Ring* and *The Two Towers* in 1954, followed by *The Return of the King* the next year). Like *The Hobbit*, *The Lord of the Rings* proved enormously popular on both sides of the Atlantic. By 1968, three million copies had sold worldwide.[7]

Both *The Hobbit* and *The Lord of the Rings*, however, presupposed the vast Middle-earth mythology Tolkien had been creating since 1917: a self-contained, internally consistent world of fantasy that was "true" because it reflected absolute reality. It evoked for Tolkien a quality of joy that was "a far-off gleam or echo of evangelium [good news; Gospel] in the real world."[8] Tolkien earnestly desired to share this mythology with the world in published form, since he believed it was crucial for a full appreciation of his fiction. *The Silmarillion,* however, would not see print until after his death. Tolkien died on September 2, 1973, in the English seaside town of Bournemouth.

J. R. R. Tolkien and Myth and "Fairy-Story"

The fiction that made him famous never mentions Jesus Christ, yet J. R. R. Tolkien remains an outstanding example of an author and thinker who—in the apostle Paul's words—"[took] captive every thought to make it obedient to Christ" (2 Corinthians 10:5). Tolkien maintained that when human writers create worlds of fantasy, such as Tolkien's own, richly imagined Middle-earth, they become "sub-creators" who reflect the activity of God, the primary Creator. In Tolkien's judgment, human creativity, especially as expressed in story-telling, is one of God's good gifts to humankind. A successful "fairy-story" set in a "secondary world"—that is, a fictional setting that nonetheless commands the belief of both reader and writer—feels "true" because fantasy "is a natural human activity" and

> remains a human right: we make in our measure and in our derivative mode, because we are made—and not only made, but made in the image and likeness of a Maker.[9]

Tolkien's work is not as *explicitly* Christian as, for example, that of his friend and colleague C. S. Lewis. Yet many readers recognize, along with poet W. H. Auden, that the "unstated presuppositions" of Tolkien's fiction are Christian.[10] Points of contact with and evocative echoes of Christian faith and practice fill these books' pages, and not by accident. Middle-earth is Tolkien's successful "sub-creation" of a world through words, and so it is a "fairy-story" reflecting God's own creation of the world through the Word, and redemption of that world through the Word made flesh (see Genesis 1:1–5; John 1:1–14). For Tolkien, the story of salvation is the

> story of a larger kind which embraces all the essence of fairy-stories . . . . [the story in which] the desire and aspiration of sub-creation has been raised to the fulfillment of Creation . . . . [T]his story is supreme; and it is true. Art has been verified. God is the Lord, of angels, and of men—and of elves. Legend and History have met and fused.[11]

Computer Link:

You can learn more about Tolkien by visiting the official web site of the Tolkien Society, a British educational charity that works "to encourage and further interest in [Tolkien's] life and works" at: www.tolkiensociety.org.

Notes

1 Humphrey Carpenter, *Tolkien: A Biography* (Boston: Houghton Mifflin Company, 1977) 176.

2 Tolkien, *The Letters of J. R. R. Tolkien,* ed. Humphrey Carpenter (1981; Boston: Houghton Mifflin Company, 2000) 219.

3 Carpenter 31.

4 Carpenter 175

5 Tolkien, *Letters* 78.

6 Carpenter 111.

7 Carpenter 182.

8 J. R. R. Tolkien, "On Fairy-stories," *The Tolkien Reader* (1966; New York: Ballantine Books, 1984) 88.

9 Tolkien, "On Fairy-stories" 74, 75.

10 Clyde S. Kilby, *Tolkien and the Silmarillion* (Wheaton, IL: Harold Shaw Publishers, 1976) 58.

11 Tolkien, "On Fairy-stories" 88, 89.

Ideas for Prereading Activities

1. If you have not already done so, read *The Fellowship of the Ring* and *The Two Towers* before studying *The Return of the King*.

2. Create a chart outlining the locations and actions of the story's major characters at the conclusion of *The Two Towers*. Consult this chart for reference, and update it as you read *The Return of the King*.

3. What qualities do you think the ideal king would possess? Consider rulers you have read about in myth, history, or legend as positive and/or negative examples. Consult the following biblical texts: 1 Kings 3:4–15; Psalm 72; Proverbs 16:10–13; 20:26; 29:14; Matthew 25:31–46.

4. Draw or copy a map of Middle-earth and use it to track the movements of the principal characters throughout the story. You may be as creative or simple as you wish in making and decorating your map. You may also wish to create a "war room" map, using pins or tags to keep track of troop movements and battles.

Book V, Chapters 1–3

Vocabulary:

For each underlined word below, choose the best definition given. Use the word's context (surrounding material) to make your choice.

1. [When Gandalf says Denethor should already have been told of Boromir's death]: "It has been guessed already," said Ingold; "for there have been strange portents here of late. . . ."

    a. omens; signs
    b. lies; falsehoods
    c. rumors; speculations

2. [The Guards'] helms gleamed with a flame of silver, for they were indeed wrought of *mithril,* heirlooms from the glory of old days . . . . This was the livery of the heirs of Elendil. . . .

    heirlooms:
    a. unhappy reminders
    b. possessions passed on from generation to generation
    c. ancient relics

    livery:
    a. distinctive dress or uniform
    b. overall appearance
    c. occupation; livelihood

3. "But you come with tidings of grief and danger, as is your <u>wont</u>, they say."

   a. strong desire
   b. urgent mission
   c. usual behavior

4. "Be careful of your words, Master Peregrin! This is no time for hobbit <u>pertness</u>."

   a. brashness
   b. shyness
   c. boldness

5. "Folly?" said Gandalf. "Nay, my lord, when you are a <u>dotard</u> you will die. . . . Do you think that I do not understand your purpose in questioning for an hour one who knows the least, while I sit by?"

   a. elderly person
   b. senile person
   c. ambitious person

6. "Few, maybe, of those now <u>sundered</u> will meet again."

   a. lost; misled
   b. separated; divided
   d. alone; isolated

7. And some said that when the Riders came from Rohan each would bring behind him a halfling warrior, small maybe, but <u>doughty</u>.

   a. strong; brave
   b. sturdy; sure-footed
   c. well-fed; well-nourished

8. "Farewell, lord!" said Aragorn. "Ride unto great <u>renown</u>!"

   a. fame; glory
   b. defeat; disgrace
   c. anonymity; obscurity

9. "Lord," she said, "if you must go, then let me ride in your following. For I am weary of <u>skulking</u> in the hills, and wish to face peril and battle."

   a. playing
   b. hiding
   c. sleeping

10. So time unreckoned passed, until Gimli saw a sight that he was ever afterwards <u>loth</u> to recall. . . . The dread was so heavy upon him that he could hardly walk.

    a. eager
    b. amused
    c. reluctant

11. . . . Merry had ridden by himself just behind the king, saying nothing, and trying to understand the slow <u>sonorous</u> speech of Rohan that he heard the men behind him using. It was a language in which there seemed to be many words that he knew, though spoken more richly and strongly than in the Shire. . . .

    a. wise; insightful
    b. deep in sound; full of tone
    c. confusing; perplexing

12. "All is well," she answered; yet it seemed to Merry that her voice <u>belied</u> her, and he would have thought that she had been weeping, if that could be believed of one so stern of face.

    a. proved false
    b. confirmed as true
    c. questioned as unreliable

13. "And he has passed into the shadow from which none have returned. I could not <u>dissuade</u> him. He is gone."

    a. deter; persuade not to
    b. cajole; trick
    c. advise; give counsel to

14. "Greatly changed he seemed to me since I saw him first . . . . grimmer, older. <u>Fey</u> I thought him, and like one whom the Dead call."

    a. fickle
    b. sensing impending death
    c. otherworldly

Characterization:

Characterization is the process by which an author establishes the distinctive traits and personalities of characters in a story. Authors use the following techniques to communicate the character attributes they wish their readers to notice:

- direct information (telling the reader something specific about the character; an older method, not much used now)
- dialogue (letting the reader infer something about the character from what the character or others say and how they say it)
- physical action (showing the character engaged in an activity that reveals something about the character)

- physical description (letting the reader infer something about the character from the character's appearance, mannerisms, and so on)
- physical surroundings (letting the reader infer something about the character from the places that character chooses to be)

In Book V, Chapter 1, we are introduced to Denethor, Steward of Minas Tirith. In the space below, quote at least one example that creates an impression of or describes Denethor for each of the techniques listed below, and briefly state what impression of Denethor the description creates.

- dialogue—

- physical action—

- physical description—

- physical surroundings—

Questions:

1. What are Pippin's first impressions of Minas Tirith? On closer inspection, what becomes apparent about the city?

2. What stands over a pool in the middle of the courtyard of the citadel of Minas Tirith? Why is it significant?

3. How did Denethor first learn about his son Boromir's death? Describe the effect Boromir's death has had upon him.

4. What motivates Pippin to offer his service to Denethor?

5. What do Gandalf and Beregond tell Pippin about Denethor's insight?

6. What news from Lebennin does Beregond tell Pippin? Why does this result in fewer men coming to the aid of Minas Tirith?

7. What gift from Galadriel does Halbarad bring to Aragorn?

8. To whom did Aragorn speak through the *palantír*, and what was that individual's response to Aragorn? Why did that individual respond as he did? Why did Aragorn use the *palantír*?

9. Who are the "Sleepless Dead"? What curse was laid upon the Dead, and why? Why does Aragorn travel the Paths of the Dead?

10. How does Merry find a way to join the march to Minas Tirith?

Thinking About the Story:

11. As they prepare to enter Denethor's great hall, Gandalf lightly rebukes Pippin for knowing nothing about the history of Gondor. Inside the hall, Gandalf pointedly rebukes Denethor for focusing almost exclusively on the good of Gondor. What do these instances have in common—in what way is Gandalf chiding Pippin and Denethor for the same thing?

12. Both Pippin and Merry pledge themselves to rulers of lands unrelated to the Shire and whom they have known only a short time. Compare and contrast the circumstances and personal reasons behind their oaths of allegiance.

13. Do you agree with Lady Éowyn's statement to Aragorn, when he refuses to allow her accompany him, that, "'All your words are but to say: you are a woman, and your part is in the house'"? Why or why not?

14. The narrator suggests that the tale he tells became the subject of "the songs of Rohan" in later years, but at the time, the subject of those songs began "without horn or harp or music of men's voices," while "many sad faces of women" looked on. What comment might Tolkien be making about the way in which wars and other events are remembered?

15. In Chapter 2, when Aragorn's party reaches Dunharrow, the language shifts into a tone very different from what Tolkien has used so far. How does the language differ from preceding paragraphs? What other kind of literature does it sound like?

From whose point of view does Tolkien tell the story after the party leaves Éowyn and enters the Paths of the Dead? Why do you think Tolkien adopts this point of view for the journey through the mountains? Why do you think Tolkien again adopts a more formal structure at the end of the chapter?

Dig Deeper:

16. The Rider Dernhelm tells Merry they have a saying, "'*Where will wants not, a way opens,*'" and then offers to carry him on the ride to Minas Tirith if he so desires. What modern saying corresponds to Dernhelm's saying?

How are the two sayings different in meaning? Do you think the sayings are true in all circumstances?

17. Both Éowyn and Merry are duty bound to remain behind when they wish to go with companions they love—both when Aragorn leaves each of them and later when Théoden rides to Minas Tirith. Do you think Merry does the right thing when he decides to secretly join Théoden's company?

18. Have you ever been torn between conflicting duties, loyalties, or obligations? How did you resolve the conflict? Read 1 Kings 3:7–12; Proverbs 3:5–7; and Romans 12:1–2. How do these scriptures help someone seeking to discern the correct course of action? What criteria should we use when deciding how to choose among competing duties, all of which may be good in their own right?

19. How might the situation of the Oathbreakers—"the Dead" who travel with the Grey Company to Pelargir upon Anduin—parallel the situation of sinful, fallen humanity as described by the apostle Paul in Romans 5 (particularly Romans 5:6, 8–11, 18, 19, 21); 6:23; and 14:9? How might Aragorn be a symbol for Christ? (Note Éowyn's words to Aragorn when he tells her he will take the Paths of the Dead and Théoden's description when Merry asks about the Paths of the Dead.)

20. In Book V, Chapter 2, Gimli is astonished and frightened when he discovers that Aragorn has looked into the Stone of Orthanc. "Even Gandalf feared that encounter," he tells Aragorn. Aragorn responds:

> "You forget to whom you speak," said Aragorn sternly, and his eyes glinted. "Did I not openly proclaim my title before the deson of Edoras? What do you fear that I should say to him? Nay, Gimli," he said in a softer voice, and the grimness left his face, and he looked like one who has laboured in sleepless pain for many nights. "Nay, my friends, I am the lawful master of the Stone, and I had both the right and the strength to use it, or so I judged. The right cannot be doubted."

Why does Aragorn respond as aggressively toward his friend as he does? Why is it more permissible for Aragorn to use the Stone than for Gandalf to use it?

Optional Activities:

1. Study the ancient tradition of the "harrowing of Hell" which especially caught the popular imagination of Christians during the Middle Ages and which continues to be an element of many Christians' faith, particularly in the Roman Catholic and Eastern Orthodox communities. How might Aragorn's gathering of the dead Oathbreakers reflect this tradition? In your presentation, include one ancient or medieval representation of the harrowing of Hell as well as a modern interpretation of it. Draw on the visual arts (paintings, sculptures) or the written word (theological texts, devotional reflections). For reference you may wish to find the apocryphal Gospel of Nicodemus, or Acts of Pilate. Pertinent scriptures include: Matthew 12:40; 27:50–54; Luke 11:21, 22; 16:23–26; Ephesians 4:7–10; Colossians 2:14, 15; Hebrews 2:14–15; 9:27, 28; 1 Peter 4:5, 6; Revelation 1:18.

2. Research stories about martyrs, ancient or modern, who have followed Christ to the point of death. Consult websites such as The Voice of the Martyrs at www.persecution.com or www.persecution.org to learn about modern persecution of Christians and possible ways Christians in this country can help their brothers and sisters in faith elsewhere. Organize a response involving your fellow students, members of your local church, or other interested and concerned persons.

3. Compare Pippin's oath of loyalty to Denethor and Merry's oath to King Théoden with the medieval practice of vassals swearing service to their lords. Research the feudal system of the Middle Ages. Present the results of your research in a creative oral and/or written form.

4. Write an opinion paper or hold a debate concerning whether it is appropriate or right for women to participate in battle. You should consider practical, cultural, and/or biblical arguments or illustrations, and make certain that your arguments are well-researched and supported. Consider modern battle situations and experiences in your arguments.

5. Read 1 Peter 3:18–22 and Bible commentaries on this passage. Write a short paper explaining the varying interpretations of the passage, and explain how Aragorn's ride through the Paths of the Dead and his encounters with the Oathbreakers may be a symbol of one of the interpretations of the passage.

Book V, Chapters 4–7

Vocabulary:

Match each of the following words to the best possible definition. You will not use all of the choices.

1. _____ livery	a.	to regret; to be sorrowful about
2. _____ to tarry	b.	to create a path; to make way
3. _____ brazier	c.	strong; firm
4. _____ dotard	d.	to linger; to loiter
5. _____ indomitable	e.	a receptacle in which to burn charcoal
6. _____ to quell	f.	a pirate
7. _____ vanguard	g.	a tight-fitting undergarment
8. _____ fey	h.	uniform; distinctive costume
9. _____ stout	i.	the leading portion; the front part
10. _____ to rue	j.	help; aid; assistance
11. _____ succour	k.	parapet; watchtower
12. _____ corsair	l.	a mound of wood on which to burn a corpse
13. _____ pyre	m.	deprived of; denied
14. _____ bereft	n.	fool; senile person
15. _____ recreant	o.	one who cares deeply
	p.	unable to be conquered; invincible
	q.	doomed to die; sensing approaching death
	r.	unfaithful; disloyal
	s.	to suppress; to put down

Literary Technique: "Archaic" Language

Authors of fiction are concerned not only with the stories they tell, but also with the ways in which they tell them. Style can matter as much as content. Throughout *The Lord of the Rings,* Tolkien writes passages in a style he himself acknowledged was "moderated or watered archaism"—that is, formal language from the past as opposed to contemporary English usage. He stated that he always felt pain

> when anyone—in an age when almost all auctorial [authorial] manhandling of English is permitted (especially if disruptive) in the name of art or 'personal expression'—immediately dismisses out of court deliberate 'archaism' . . . . Shake yourself out of this parochialism of time! [Tolkien, *Letters* 225–226]

Notice Tolkien's use of "archaism" in, for example, Chapter 6, "The Battle of the Pelennor Fields." What examples can you find? Why do you think Tolkien has switched to a more archaic usage of English? What effect do you think he hoped to produce? Does it, in fact, produce that effect for you as a reader?

At what other points in the trilogy have you noted archaic language? How does it contrast with other styles Tolkien employs to tell his tale? Why do you think Tolkien varied his style so often?

Questions:

1. What news does Faramir bring that is of special interest to Gandalf and Pippin? Why does Denethor seem displeased by this news? What previous incident makes Denethor's displeasure ironic?

2. Sauron begins his attack on Gondor sooner than Gandalf and the men of Gondor expected. What does Gandalf speculate is the reason for Sauron's sudden move?

3. How does Gandalf respond to Pippin's concern that Frodo and Sam are with Gollum?

4. Who is the "chief captain" of the armies of Mordor, and to what legend "of old" about his fate does Gandalf refer? How is this prophecy later realized in battle?

5. What happens to Faramir in battle, and how does Denethor respond?

6. Who are the Woses, and how do they help the Rohirrim? Briefly characterize the relationship of the Woses and the people of Gondor.

7. Why has Denethor not received news of the Rohirrim's coming to Minas Tirith?

8. What is the "flaw" in the Lord of the Nazgûl's plans to which the narrator alludes?

9. Whom do the men of Minas Tirith think sail aboard the ships from Umbar? Who actually sails on them?

Thinking About the Story:

10. How does putting on "the livery and gear of the Tower" symbolize a change in Pippin's character and role in the early portion of Chapter 4? How does the text suggest Pippin feels about his new role? Have you ever had a similar moment of realization or a sudden shift in perspective? If so, how did it affect you?

11. When Pippin sees Gandalf coming to the rescue of Faramir early in Chapter 4, he says, "He always turns up when things are darkest. Go on! Go on, White Rider!" What biblical allusion might Tolkien be making with the image of a white rider? How would such an allusion affect the passage?

12. Describe the relationship between Denethor and Faramir. What are its strengths? What are its weaknesses? Does their relationship "ring true" to you?

Why or why not? Have you known parents and children who struggle with similar issues? How did they resolve these issues, if they were able?

13. Both Aragorn and Denethor use a *palantír* and, through it, challenge Sauron. What makes Aragorn's use of the Seeing Stone acceptable, while Denethor's use of a *palantír* is dangerous? What might the difference between them teach us not only about their characters but also about the importance of knowing one's own limits?

14. Reread the last paragraph of Chapter 5. What is distinctive about the rhythms and language of the last half of this paragraph, beginning with the words, "His golden shield was uncovered"? Is the grammar of these sentences considered "good writing"? Why do you think Tolkien wrote in this way? What image or feeling do you get from the passage? It may help to read this passage aloud.

Dig Deeper:

15. Some of the people of Minas Tirith place great confidence in the strength of their city. As the armies of Mordor besiege it, they do not fear because "the main wall of the City was of great height and marvellous thickness . . . and its outward face was . . . unconquerable by steel or fire, unbreakable except by some convulsion that would rend the very earth on which it stood." Compare the people's confidence in their city with the confidence expressed by the people of Jerusalem in Psalm 48. How is it similar? How is it different? How does

Psalm 46 use language about a strong city to teach us where we should place our ultimate confidence?

16. The narrator tells us that Sauron uses "dread and despair" as weapons in his war against the races of the West. Why are dread and despair so terrible? Read the story of the siege of Samaria in 2 Kings 6:24–7:20. What parallels can you draw between the biblical story and Tolkien's story of the siege of Minas Tirith? Do these stories give us alternatives to despair?

17. What are the consequences of Denethor's despair? Why do you think despair is often considered a sin in Christian thought? (Consider the common thread linking Genesis 18:14, Matthew 16:24–26, and Luke 1:37.) How do texts such as Psalm 130, John 16:33, and 2 Corinthians 4:7–10 present an alternative to despair? (See also Philippians 3:7, 8; Romans 8:18–21, 24–28, 31, 35–39.)

Have you ever felt despair or a similar emotion? How did you deal it? How did the situation look to you later, after it had passed? What would you say to someone feeling despair?

18. Pippin challenges Beregond with a duty higher than that given him by Denethor: "Well, you must choose between orders and the life of Faramir." How does Beregond's choice mirror the choice faced by the Lady Éowyn in Chapter 2? How might Pippin's words to him relate to Jesus' words to the Pharisees in Matthew 12:1–14?

19. As Denethor prepares to immolate himself and Faramir, Gandalf tells Denethor, "Authority is not given to you, Steward of Gondor, to order the hour of your death." Yet Denethor insists that Gandalf "shall not defy my will: to rule my own end." What fatal character flaw does Denethor's statement reveal? What do the following biblical texts teach about that flaw: Proverbs 8:13; 16:18; 29:23; Isaiah 2:11, 17; 13:11; Daniel 4:37; Matthew 5:3; Luke 1:51–53? What attitude does Jesus instruct his followers to take, in contrast to Denethor's, when they pray (see Matthew 6:10 and Luke 11:2)?

20. Although Denethor was never fully "subdued to the will of the Dark Power" when he used the *palantír*, Gandalf says the Steward was nonetheless "deceived." How was Denethor deceived? Do you see examples of this type of deception practiced today? If so, list some examples or situations in which you see such deception. How can we guard ourselves against similar deception?

21.   In Chapter 1 Pippin and Beregond have the following conversation:

> [Beregond] "This is a great war long-planned, and we are but one piece in it, whatever pride may say. . . . And now all realms shall be put to the test, to stand, or fall—under the Shadow.
>
> "Yet, Master Peregrin, we have this honour: ever we bear the brunt of the chief hatred of the Dark Lord, . . . Here will the hammer-stroke fall hardest. And for that reason Mithrandir came hither in such haste. For if we fall, who shall stand? And, Master Peregrin, do you see any hope that we shall stand?"
>
> . . . .
>
> [Pippin] "No, my heart will not yet despair. . . . We may stand, if only on one leg, or at least be left still upon our knees."
>
> "Rightly said!" cried Beregond, rising and striding to and fro. "Nay, though all things must come utterly to an end in time, Gondor shall not perish yet. . . . There are still other fastnesses, and secret ways of escape into the mountains. Hope and memory shall live still in some hidden valley where the grass is green."

Contrast Beregond's perspective of Gondor's place in the world with Denethor's, giving specific examples from the text. Which perspective do you think gave greater solace and perseverance? Why?

Read 1 Kings 19:1–18. What was Elijah's primary complaint and problem? What was God's answer? How is Denethor similar to Elijah in this passage?

22. *Hubris* refers to excessive pride, arrogance, and/or insolence resulting in the downfall of the person possessing it. *Hamartia* refers to an action that leads to the downfall of a hero. The action may be due to an error in judgment, a character flaw, ignorance, or accident. Which of these terms do you think best describes Denethor's fall, or do you think Denethor suffers from a combination of the two? Give examples from the text to support your answer. If you see hamartia, describe the moment it occurs.

Optional Activities:

1. Research the experiences of the Aborigines in Australia under European rule, and compare those experiences with the relationship between the Woses and the Rohirrim. Present your findings in a three- to five-page paper or an oral report.

2. At the beginning of Chapter 4, Pippin dons the livery and gear of Minas Tirith. Research the articles of clothing and armor Pippin receives, then put together a presentation explaining or illustrating the items. You may create a picture or painting illustrating Pippin in his new attire, create a poster illustrating and describing the various items and their purposes, or create examples of the clothing and/or armor and explain how it was used.

3. Compare the relationship between Denethor and Faramir with the relationship between Saul and Jonathan as recorded in 1 Samuel 19, 20, and 31. Write a short paper detailing the similarities and noting the differences between these two pairs of fathers and sons and their relationships.

4. Throughout literature, prophecy has been a two-edged sword. On the one hand, it often gives guidance to characters in how to act or what to expect. On the other hand, prophecy is rarely as clear as it seems, and characters often are brought down by relying on prophecy they have taken too literally.

In the middle of Chapter 4, as Gandalf and Denethor discuss the Lord of the Nazgûl, Gandalf says, "'And if words spoken of old be true, not by the hand of man shall he fall, and hidden from the Wise is the doom that awaits him.'" In Chapter 6, as the Lord of the Nazgûl stands over Théoden, he says to Dernhelm, "'Hinder me? Thou fool. No living man may hinder me!'" Of course, the Nazgûl Lord has applied the prophecy too broadly, to his own doom.

Write a paper comparing the above events with the witches' prophecies concerning Macbeth, particularly those found in Act 4, Scene 1, and Act 5, Scenes 5 and 8, of the play by Shakespeare. How do Tolkien and Shakespeare use prophecy in similar ways and what are the consequences? Can you find any other similar instances of prophecy and consequences in literature? Do you think there are similar dangers in interpreting scriptural prophecy? Use specific references to text to illustrate your positions throughout your paper.

Book V, Chapters 8–10

Vocabulary:

Match the following clues with the appropriate words from the Word Box to complete the crossword puzzle on the next page.

Word Box

abate	furled	staunch	doggrel	trammel
tryst	noisome	feint	wizened	surety
bandy	base	bode	clemency	proffered

Down

1. shriveled; withered
2. pledge; guarantee
4. rolled up
5. crude or poor poetry
7. offensive or toxic in odor
8. to stop blood flow
11. to toss or throw back and forth

Across

3. offered; extended for acceptance or rejection
6. a feigned or deceptive movement
9. to make an appointment; to set a meeting
10. to reduce; to decrease
11. common; vulgar
12. mercy

Questions:

1. How is Merry suffering as a result of his encounter with the Lord of the Nazgûl?

2. What piece of lore does Ioreth remember that gives hope for those who suffer in the Houses of Healing?

3. What is *athelas*? What is its importance? How does Ioreth describe its appearance and aroma? Where else in *The Lord of the Rings* series did we encounter *athelas*?

4. What does Gandalf tell Éomer was the true beginning of his sister Éowyn's malady?

5. By what name do the people of Minas Tirith call Aragorn after he heals many? What is significant about this name?

6. Why does Gandalf counsel Aragorn and his fellow Captains to attack the forces of Sauron?

7. According to Gandalf, how will the destruction of the Ring ensure the destruction of Sauron?

8. Why, according to what Aragorn tells Merry, should Pippin "represent the Shirefolk" in the final battle against Sauron? How does Aragorn put Pippin's presence at the battle in perspective for Merry?

9. What does Imrahil urge the army's heralds to cry as they advance into Mordor? Why?

10. What is Pippin's contribution in the last battle at the Black Gate?

Thinking About the Story:

11. In your opinion, who is the wiser: Ioreth or the herb-master? Why? What conclusions might you draw from the way Tolkien treats these two characters about the relative importance of academic knowledge and practical knowledge (direct personal knowledge or folk wisdom)?

12. Reflecting on their respective services to Denethor and Théoden, Pippin tells Merry, "We Tooks and Brandybucks, we can't live long on the heights." Merry replies, "But at least . . . we can now see them, and honour them. It is best to love first what you are fitted to love, I suppose: you must start somewhere and

have some roots, and the soil of the Shire is deep." In your own words, what would you say Merry means? Do you agree with him? Why or why not?

13. As he advises Aragorn and the other captains to attack Sauron, Gandalf uses an extended metaphor to put their efforts in perspective. Explain the metaphor he uses. What does Gandalf mean? Do you agree with his opinion? Would you characterize it as optimistic, pessimistic, realistic, or in some other way? Why do you react as you do? To what contemporary situations could you apply Gandalf's judgment?

14. Who is "the Mouth of Sauron?" What might his lack of a personal identity reveal about Tolkien's view of evil? What other evidence from *The Lord of the Rings* could you site to support your conclusion?

15. What tokens does the Mouth of Sauron display to the Captains of the West? What does he say they mean? What conclusions can the reader draw from his words?

16. What leads Pippin to think he understands "poor Denethor a little better"? How do they differ in their final decisions?

Dig Deeper:

17. What are some of the images and language the narrator uses to describe the fragrance of *athelas*? What impression do these images and language give? Compare these images and languages to those found in Hosea 14:4–8; 2 Corinthians 2:14–16; and Ephesians 5:1–2. What do the images in these passages describe, and how are they similar to the language used of *athelas*? What connections, if any, can you make between the biblical language and Tolkien's language?

18. In Chapter 9, as Aragorn heals Faramir, onlookers feel that Aragorn "walk[s] afar in some dark vale, calling for one that [is] lost." Aragorn tells Faramir, "Walk no more in the shadows, but awake!" He says he perhaps has power to heal Éowyn's body and "to recall her from the dark valley." He later tells Pippin that he has "called [Merry] back" from the threat of death. Read Psalm 23 and John 10:27–30. How does the language used of Aragorn as healer parallel these passages?

19. Read Mark 5:35–43, Matthew 8:14–17; 15:29–31, and Ephesians 5:14. What further parallels can you draw between Jesus and Aragorn after reading these scriptures?

20. Aragorn tells Pippin that Merry will not forget his grief, "but it will not darken his heart, it will teach him wisdom." What does Aragorn mean? How can grief teach us wisdom? How does 2 Corinthians 7:8–13a relate to Aragorn's statement?

21. Legolas says that Aragorn's company's journey on the Paths of the Dead will remain a great deed "though none be left in Gondor to sing of it in the days that are to come." What makes a deed great? Gandalf tells Merry that he may have great deeds to do in the final defense of Minas Tirith if their army falls in the attack on Mordor—would such a defense be a great deed, even if hopeless? Do you agree with Legolas that the rightness or greatness of a deed does not depend upon others recognizing it? Explain your answers.

Read Matthew 6:1; 1 Corinthians 10:31; Colossians 3:17, and 1 Peter 4:11. How do these scriptures fit into the discussion above?

22. Review Aragorn's actions after he arrives at Minas Tirith. Are they what you would expect from one who is the rightful king? How do Aragorn's actions compare or contrast with Matthew 20:25–28 and Luke 22:25, 26? Cite specific examples from the text in your answer.

Overview Essays for Book V

1. In an essay of three to five pages, compare and contrast Pippin's service to Denethor and Merry's service to King Théoden. What do the similarities and differences tell us about the two hobbits? About the men whom they serve? About the cultures in which they find themselves?

2. Duty—"doing one's part"—is one important theme in Book V. In an essay of three to five pages, explore the struggles one of the following characters faces as he or she seeks to do his or her part: Merry, Pippin, Éowyn, Aragorn, or Faramir. Include some personal reflections on how this character's choices and contributions to the cause are relevant to you.

3. Tolkien carefully uses light and dark imagery throughout Book V. In an essay of three to five pages, trace his references to and depiction of light and darkness, explaining how they illustrate the plot and/or the characters. How can Tolkien's use of this imagery contribute to your interpretation of his work?

4. Denethor, Pippin, and Gandalf in different ways discuss choosing how their lives will end. In a short paper, compare and contrast how these three characters discuss their choices and how they act when they think their deaths may be inevitable.

Book VI, Chapters 1–4

Vocabulary:

Read the following sentences carefully, paying attention to the underlined vocabulary words. Identify which sentences use the vocabulary words incorrectly, and write an original sentence indicating your understanding of the word in question.

1. The <u>welter</u> of the Atlantic Ocean tossed the fragile schooner about in the storm as though it were a child's bath toy.

   _____ Correct   _____ Incorrect

   Sentence:

2. Your decision to join this organization is <u>irrevocable</u>—once you're in, you're a member for life.

   _____ Correct   _____ Incorrect

   Sentence:

3. She opened the small box beneath the Christmas tree, saw the pearl earrings she had been eyeing in the store window for months, and was <u>aghast</u> with joy.

   _____ Correct   _____ Incorrect

   Sentence:

4. Harry heard the joke, understood it, and, greatly <u>bemused</u>, let loose with a long, hearty belly laugh, adding his voice to the already boisterous <u>din</u> of the party.

bemused

_____ Correct   _____ Incorrect

Sentence:

din

_____ Correct   _____ Incorrect

Sentence:

5. Nana is a real <u>bastion</u> of support because she can always be counted upon to help you through a tough time.

_____ Correct   _____ Incorrect

Sentence:

6. Seeing how much smaller his piece of pie was than the pieces everyone else at the table had received, Carl complained, "Hey, Dad—you <u>stinted</u> me!"

_____ Correct   _____ Incorrect

Sentence:

7. "They call it Danger Bay," the old fisherman explained, "because so many <u>vassals</u> have <u>foundered</u> before reaching shore."

vassals

_____ Correct   _____ Incorrect

Sentence:

foundered

_____ Correct   _____ Incorrect

Sentence:

8. The baby's appetite was <u>insatiable</u>, and so he drank only half his bottle.

_____ Correct   _____ Incorrect

Sentence:

9. Anita was <u>beleaguered</u> by flies, and spent the entire picnic swatting them away from her head.

_____ Correct   _____ Incorrect

Sentence:

10. The lawyer served me a <u>lay</u> which ordered me to appear in court on October 25. (noun)

_____ Correct   _____ Incorrect

Sentence:

11. Sancho Panza was Don Quixote's <u>esquire</u>.

   _____ Correct   _____ Incorrect

   Sentence:

12. The <u>serried</u> warriors dotted the battlefield here and there, keeping a safe distance from each other as they advanced.

   _____ Correct   _____ Incorrect

   Sentence:

Narrative Technique: Interlacing

As Book VI begins, the narrator calls our attention to the fact that, while the events we are reading about are unfolding, the events we have read about in Book V are taking place simultaneously. As Sam decides to enter Cirith Ungol, for instance, the narrator tells us that "even now Aragorn was leading the black fleet from Pelargir, and Merry was riding with the Rohirrim down the Stonewain Valley, while in Minas Tirith flames were rising and Pippin watched the madness growing in the eyes of Denethor." As Frodo and Sam approach the end of their journey to Mount Doom, the narrator tells us that only the Nazgûl could have warned Sauron, but "the Nazgûl and their black wings were abroad on other errand . . . shadowing the march of the Captains of the West . . . ." Critic Tom Shippey calls this technique "interlacing"— "several . . . threads [of story], twisted round each other, [to] make up a saga." [Tom Shippey, *J. R. R. Tolkien: Author of the Century* (Boston: Houghton Mifflin, 2001) 103.] The technique appears elsewhere in *The Lord of the Rings* as well: for example, throughout the early chapters of Book III, as we shift our attention back and forth between Aragorn, Gimli, and Legolas; and Merry and Pippin. Consult Appendix B, "The Great Years," for help in determining more examples of interlacing.

   Why do you think Tolkien structured so much of his story using this technique? What advantages for story-telling does it offer? What disadvantages? What effects do you think it is designed to have on the reader? Does it increase your appreciation for the story? Why or why not?

Alliteration and Assonance:

Alliteration is the repetition of consonant sounds either at the beginning of words or within words. *Assonance* is the repetition of vowel sounds within words. Both techniques give a passage a lyrical quality. In the paragraph below, underline instances of alliteration and cross out instances of assonance. Remember that both techniques use repeated *sounds,* not necessarily the same letter.

> All was ominously quiet. The light was no more than that of dusk at a dark day's end. The vast vapours that arose in Mordor and went streaming westward passed low overhead, a great welter of cloud and smoke now lit again beneath with a sullen glow of red.

Questions:

1. How does Sam make his way past the Two Watchers at the gate of Cirith Ungol? How do he and Frodo escape them when leaving Cirith Ungol, and what happens to the Watchers then?

2. How does Frodo react when he learns that Sam has the Ring? What does this imply about Frodo or the Ring? [If you have read *The Fellowship of the Ring,* to what other event is this similar?]

3. What does Shagrat carry away with him that will cause much grief, though not to Sam or Frodo?

4. What do Frodo and Sam see and hear on the morning of March 15th that causes Sam to feel renewed hope? What do we, as readers, know about these things that these characters do not?

5. How do Sam and Frodo get across the plains of Mordor undetected?

6. Why is Sam unable to kill Gollum on the Road to the Sammath Naur?

7. What happens to the Ring after Frodo puts it on at the Cracks of Doom?

8. How do Frodo and Sam escape the destruction of Mount Doom? Where do they go?

Thinking About the Story:

9. These chapters contain several parallels to situations found in scripture. Look up each of the scriptures below, then briefly describe the incident or situation from the book that comes closest to being a parallel to the scripture.

    a. Genesis 37:28, 36; 45:4–7:

    b. Genesis 37:31–35:

    c. Matthew 4:1–10 [Luke 4:1–13]:

10. *Anthropomorphism* is the giving of human characteristics to a nonhuman object or creature. (Anthropomorphism is often confused with *personification,* which is embodying an idea or concept in human form, such as Jiminy Cricket personifying a conscience in the Disney *Pinnochio* movie.) Underline the words in the following passage that illustrate anthropomorphism, then explain what tone they give the passage and how Tolkien uses the anthropomorphic words to help create the tone.

    > And here things still grew, harsh, twisted, bitter, struggling for life. In the glens of the Morgai on the other side of the valley low scrubby trees lurked and clung, coarse grey grass-tussocks fought with the stones, and withered mosses crawled on them; and everywhere great writhing, tangled brambles sprawled.

11. *Irony* is a difference between appearance and reality, or between what is expected and what actually occurs. There are a number of ironies in the circumstances of the destruction of the Ring. Describe at least two and explain why they are ironic.

12. In *The Two Towers,* Book IV, Chapter 1, when Gollum wishes to swear on the Ring that he will be trustworthy, Frodo responds,

    "On the Precious? How dare you?" he said. "Think!

    One Ring to rule them all and in the Darkness bind them.

    Would you commit your promise to that, Sméagol? It will hold you. But it is more treacherous than you are. It may twist your words. Beware!"

    Later, in Chapter 3 of the same book, as Gollum tries to dissuade Frodo and Sam from entering the gates of Mordor and offers to take the burden from Frodo or show them a different way into Mordor, Frodo says,

    "*Give it back to Sméagol* you said. Do not say that again! Do not let that thought grow in you! You will never get it back. But the desire of it may betray you to a bitter end. You will never get it back. In the last need, Sméagol, I should put on the Precious; and the Precious mastered you long ago. If I, wearing it, were to command you, you would obey, even if it were to leap from a precipice or to cast yourself into the fire. And such would be my command. So have a care, Sméagol!"

    And, of course, at the end, on the side of Mount Doom as Frodo and Sam are nearing their goal when Gollum attacks them, Frodo tells Gollum,

    "Begone and trouble me no more! If you touch me ever again, you shall be cast yourself into the Fire of Doom."

Do you think these passages are foreshadowing or careful plotting by Tolkien? Knowing the nature of the Ring, do you think Gollum's end was an ironic accident, a natural (but not inevitable) result of circumstances, or the direct result of an evolving (though unconscious) command—or curse—by Frodo?

13. As noted in the "About the Author" section of this study guide, Tolkien insisted that successful "fairy-story" reflected a reality greater than itself, a truth that transcends the "sub-creation" in which the fairy-story is set. This transcendent truth gives the fairy-story its consoling function—commonly called "the Happy Ending." But Tolkien called this narrative moment the *eucatastrophe*—literally, the "good catastrophe":

    > The consolation of fairy-stories, the joy of the happy ending: or more correctly of the good catastrophe, the sudden joyous "turn" . . . this joy, which is one of the things which fairy-stories can produce supremely well, is not essentially "escapist," nor "fugitive." In its fairy-tale—or otherworld—setting, it is a sudden and miraculous grace: never to be counted on to recur. It does not deny the existence of *dyscatastrophe,* of sorrow and failure: the possibility of these is necessary to the joy of deliverance; it denies (in the face of much evidence, if you will) universal final defeat and in so far is *evangelium,* giving a fleeting glimpse of Joy, Joy beyond the walls of the world, poignant in grief. [J. R. R. Tolkien, "On Fairy-stories," *The Tolkien Reader* (New York: Ballantine Books, 1966): 85–86.]

    Given this discussion, evaluate the scene in which Sam awakens in Ithilien as a moment of *eucatastrophe.* How does this scene meet or fail to meet the characteristics Tolkien outlines above?

14. From whose point of view is this section predominately presented? Why do you think Tolkien decided to approach these chapters from this character's viewpoint?

Dig Deeper:

15. Describe the specific temptation Sam faces when he puts on the Ring at Cirith Ungol. What similarities or differences do you see between this temptation scene and the temptations of Jesus as recorded in Matthew 4:1–11 and Luke 4:1–13? What do Sam and Jesus' temptations suggest about the right and wrong uses of power? Consult Matthew 20:20–28 when thinking about your answer.

16. What does Sam see high above the Ephel Dúath one night that changes his perspective on his and Frodo's circumstances? How does his perspective change?

    Read Psalm 102:25–27; Isaiah 57:15; John 1:5, 16:33; Hebrews 1:10–12, 13:8. How might these verses provide Christians with an experience similar to Sam's? To what "light" should Christians turn—what is eternal and secure?

17. Tolkien once wrote that lembas serves two functions in *The Lord of the Rings*. It is a "device for making credible the long marches with little provisions," and it has "what one might hesitatingly call a 'religious'" function: "This becomes later apparent, especially in the chapter 'Mount Doom.'" [Tolkien, *Letters* 275] Based on the description of lembas in that chapter, what might its "religious" function or significance be? Read John 6:27, 48–51 and 1 Corinthians 10:14–22. How might *lembas* be similar to or different from the bread discussed in these biblical texts?

18. Just like Isildur (see *The Fellowship of the Ring*, Book II, Chapter 2), Frodo chooses to not destroy the Ring. In a draft of a letter to one of his readers, Tolkien offers this commentary on the end of the Quest:

   "No, Frodo 'failed' . . . . [O]ne must face the fact: the power of Evil in the world is *not* finally resistible by incarnate creatures, however 'good'; and the Writer of the Story is not one of us." [Tolkien, *Letters* 252.]

   What do you think Tolkien meant? How does the scene at the Cracks of Doom support your answer? How *is* "the power of Evil in the world" overcome—not only in Middle-earth, but also in our world today? Read Matthew 6:13—a text Tolkien himself suggested was critical for interpreting Frodo's "failure"—and Romans 7:15–25 when considering your response.

Optional Activities:

1. Sam realizes, as he looks at Cirith Ungol, that the great tower fortress had been built by Gondor, "not to keep enemies out of Mordor, but to keep them in." Now that the stronghold had fallen into Sauron's hands, "still its chief purpose as of old was to prevent escape from Mordor," for Sauron "had few servants but many slaves of fear."

   Research the Berlin Wall and write a two- to three-page paper describing its creation, purpose, history, and final destruction.

2. Write your own song or poem of victory and praise for Sam and Frodo. You may wish to read Exodus 15:1–18 and Judges 5 for biblical examples of such songs.

3. Using watercolors or colored pencils, create a picture of Sam and Frodo recuperating under the beech grove in Ithilien.

Book VI, Chapters 5–6

Vocabulary:

For each of the following words, write your definition. Then check your definition against that given in a standard dictionary.

1. *gainsaid*
   Your Definition:

   Dictionary Definition:

2. *puissant*
   Your Definition:

   Dictionary Definition:

3. *renown*
   Your Definition:

   Dictionary Definition:

4. *palfrey*
   Your Definition:

   Dictionary Definition:

5. *niggard*
   Your Definition:

   Dictionary Definition:

Questions:

1. Why does Lady Éowyn feel not fully healed in the Houses of Healing? What, according to the Warden of the Houses, eventually brings about her full healing?

2. How does Aragorn respond when Faramir attempts to relinquish the office of Steward?

3. Whom does Aragorn wish to crown him, and why?

4. How does Aragorn deal with Beregond?

5. Why does Aragorn want the members of the Fellowship to remain in Minas Tirith?

6. What charge does Gandalf give to Aragorn on Mount Mindolluin?

7. What does Aragorn see in the snow on Mount Mindolluin, and why is it significant?

8. What is "the choice of Lúthien" to which Arwen refers, which she has made, and which accounts for her inability to travel to the Grey Havens with Elrond? (If necessary, refer back to Book I, Chapter 11, the song and explanation near the chapter end.) Who will travel to the Havens with Elrond instead of Arwen?

9. What gift does Arwen give Frodo?

10. What event unites Gondor and Rohan more closely?

11. What gift does Éowyn give to Merry? What is its significance?

12. How was Saruman able to leave Orthanc?

13. What thinly veiled warning does Saruman give to Gandalf and the hobbits as they journey toward the Shire?

Thinking About the Story:

14. In what sense might the fall of Sauron as it is experienced by the citizens of Minas Tirith be a moment of *eucatastrophe*, as defined in the previous section (Question 13)?

15. In response to a reader's criticism that the relationship between Faramir and Éowyn develops too quickly, Tolkien wrote, "In my experience feelings and decisions ripen very quickly (as measured by mere 'clock-time', which is actually not justly applicable) in periods of great stress, and especially under the expectation of imminent death." [Tolkien, *Letters* 324] Do you agree with Tolkien? In your opinion, how satisfactory is Tolkien's portrayal of Éowyn and Faramir's relationship?

16. *Comic relief* is a term referring to a humorous scene or exchange introduced into a serious scene or work to ease the tension (*relief* with the connotation of alleviating or easing) or to contrast with the drama of the scene and so heighten its effect (*relief* with the connotation of being physically low and contrasting with something physically high; bas-relief). In the middle of Chapter 5, what exchange during Aragorn's procession into Minas Tirith stands out as comic relief? Why do you think Tolkien interjects these exchanges into what is otherwise a solemn and stately passage?

17. Why do you think Saruman reacts as he does to Gandalf and the hobbits when they meet him in the forest at the feet of the Misty Mountains? What generalizations about unhealthy self-pride (*hubris*) can you draw from the specific instance of Saruman's behavior at this point? What experiences have you had, or can you draw from other sources, to support your conclusions?

Quite often, what one suspects of others is what one would be tempted to do oneself under the same circumstances. What does this say about Saruman's difficulty seeing the kindness and mercy of Gandalf and the hobbits?

18. Why do you think Wormtongue refuses to leave Saruman, even now in his defeat? Do you find Wormtongue sympathetic or not at this point? Do you agree with Gandalf that it should be just as simple as "Then leave him!" for Wormtongue to escape his situation? Have you seen examples of this dynamic at work in your own or others' experience?

19. As the hobbits; Elrond and his people; Celeborn, Galadriel, and their people; and Gandalf pause in their journey near the gates of Moria, Gandalf and the elves "lingered in converse. . . . under the stars, recalling the ages that were gone and all their joys and labours in the world," appearing as "grey figures, carved in stone, memorials of forgotten things now lost in unpeopled lands." To what image in Book V, Chapter 3, is this image of the characters carved in stone parallel or reminiscent? What does this scene and the parallel scene seem to imply about Gandalf and the elves?

Dig Deeper:

20. At the beginning of Chapter 5, Éowyn tells the Warden of the Houses of Healing, "'it is not always good to be healed in body. Nor is it always evil to die in battle, even in bitter pain. Were I permitted, in this dark hour I would choose the latter.'" Is there a difference between choosing to commit suicide and choosing to not keep one's body alive? Do you agree with Éowyn that in some circumstances sometimes it is better to not be healed or saved from death?

    In Éowyn's circumstance, considering what comes later in these chapters, would it have been better for her to be allowed to die on the battlefield? If she could have seen what was in her future, do you think she would have said, "'Were I permitted, in this dark hour I would choose the latter [death on the battlefield]'"?

21. Critic Tom Shippey notes that the song of the great Eagle—a song of "tidings beyond hope"—resembles a biblical psalm. Compare the Eagle's song with Psalms 2, 23, 24, 47, 48, 61, and 98. What similarities do you notice? What differences? Why might Tolkien have chosen to compose a psalm at this point in his story? How might this choice reflect his Christian faith?

22. When Faramir asks Aragorn to be relieved of the office of Steward, Aragorn responds, "That office is not ended, and it shall be thine and thy heirs' as long as my line shall last." Why do you think Aragorn wishes to see the office of Steward continued? What misconception about stewardship might Faramir have had (a misconception taken to its extreme by his father; see Book V,

Chapter 4)? What is true stewardship? Read Ephesians 2:8–10 and Matthew 5:13–16. What do these texts suggest about the responsibility of Christians to be stewards for King Jesus?

23. Read Daniel 7:9, 10; Revelation 1:12–18; 21:3–7. From the context of these verses, to whom are they referring and what are the circumstances? Reread, near the end of Chapter 5, the description of the crowning of Aragorn, from the moment Gandalf places the crown on his head to the moment the trumpets sound. What allusions do you see in this passage to the scriptures above? What impression do you think Tolkien wants to give to the reader by making these allusions?

24. How do you react to the kindness that Gandalf and the hobbits attempt to express to Saruman? Do you think that Saruman is worthy of their pity? Read Luke 6:36; Romans 5:6–8; 1 Corinthians 13:5–6; Colossians 3:13. What motivates a Christian to show pity or mercy to others? According to these verses, can a Christian ever say that someone "doesn't deserve" mercy and kindness? How should Christians react when their attempts at mercy and kindness are rebuffed, as Saruman rebuffs the attempts Gandalf and the hobbits make? Read Matthew 10:11–14 for guidance.

25. The passing, or ending, of the Third Age of Middle-earth is a strong theme in *The Lord of the Rings*. What illustrations of this passing do you find in these chapters? How do you handle transitions or things ending in your life? How does scripture help us confront changes and endings in the world and our own

lives? Consider such texts as Genesis 3:19; Psalm 90; Ecclesiastes 3:1–14; 12:1–7; Isaiah 25:6–8; and 1 Corinthians 7:31; 15:20–28, 50–57.

Optional Activities:

1. Read John 18:33–19:16. Write a short paper comparing and contrasting this passage with the crowning of Aragorn. In what ways are the actions of Pilate and the soldiers a parody of a royal coronation (also, read the King James Version [esp. John 19:5])? From what Jesus says in this text, why did he allow himself to suffer this abuse? You may wish to expand upon this with text from other scriptures.

2. Research living wills (sometimes called health care advance directives) and health care power of attorney in your location or state. You may wish to interview an ethics specialist from your local hospital or clinic for a health care perspective and your pastor for his spiritual perspective. Write a paper or create a presentation explaining the function and form of living wills and your conclusions about what yours would say. Use scripture in reaching and supporting your conclusions. Remember to credit your sources.

3. For a more modern idea of the pageantry of a coronation, view a videotape of Queen Elizabeth II's coronation, June 2, 1953. You may also wish to view a tape of the wedding of Prince Charles and Princess Diana of Great Britain for an idea of a royal wedding. Such segments may be found in materials about Queen Elizabeth II, the British royal family, or recent histories of Britain.

Book VI, Chapters 7–9

Vocabulary:

Replace each of the underlined words in the following sentences with a word from the Word Box. You will not use all of the choices.

	Word Box		
insolent	cudgel	uncanny	errantry
ruffian	gangrels	daunt	abashed

1. Susan decided to confront the <u>rude</u> (_____)
    <u>bully</u> (_____) who was threatening her at school.

2. It's <u>strange</u> (_____) that the twins, though separated at birth and
    having lived their lives on opposite coasts of the country, still share so many of
    the same mannerisms, interests, and attitudes.

3. I am <u>embarrassed</u> (_____) by my thoughtless, reckless behavior.

4. Mount Everest's height did not in the least <u>discourage</u> (_____)
    Tallahassee Tom, world-famous explorer, who was intent upon scaling it.

Questions:

1. When Gandalf and the hobbits arrive at The Prancing Pony, what are some of the first signs that the situation at home has changed since they left?

2. How would you describe the mood that has come over Bree since Gandalf and the hobbits were last there?

3. Why will Gandalf not accompany the hobbits to the Shire?

4. Who is "the Chief," and what effect has he had on life in the Shire?

5. What has happened to Hobbiton in Frodo's and Sam's absence?

6. According to Farmer Cotton, when did life in the Shire begin to change?

7. How does Merry rouse the hobbits in Hobbiton?

8. Who is "Sharkey"?

9. Why does Frodo refuse to have Saruman slain?

10. What are the fates of Lotho, Saruman, and Wormtongue?

11. How does Sam use his gift from Galadriel?

12. What is the significance of Frodo falling ill on particular days each year? What is the significance of Frodo's recovery on March 25, 1420, and the birth of Elanor Gamgee on March 25, 1421?

13. To where do Bilbo, Frodo, Gandalf, and the Elves depart?

Thinking About the Story:

14. *Irony* is the difference between appearance and reality, or between what is expected and what actually occurs, but it can also be the difference between what characters mistakenly believe to be true and what the reader knows to be true. For instance Butterbur is shocked and dismayed that five residents of Bree were killed in skirmishes during the winter. However, the reader knows, as Gandalf says, that Bree has "been on the edge of very great troubles, and I am only glad to hear that you have not been deeper in"—in other words, Bree's misfortunes are small compared to what the travellers have seen and other populations have suffered. Butterbur's comments about the terrible times Bree has suffered are ironic because they know Bree's trials were minor compared to those suffered by much of Middle-earth. List three other instances of irony found in these chapters.

15. Near the end of Chapter 8, Saruman says of Gandalf:

     "When his tools have done their task he drops them. But you must go dangling after him, dawdling and talking, and riding round twice as far as you needed."

     What is ironic about this statement, particularly when viewed with subsequent events?

16. *Parochialism* refers to a provincial or narrow outlook on life, generally restricted to one's own experiences or geographical region. (*Parochial* refers to a parish.) An example of parochialism would be Butterbur saying "'we don't want no outsiders at Bree, nor near Bree at all. We want to be let alone,'" and not being able to imagine why the King would care about Bree at all, much less being able to understand that Strider is the King. Describe two other instances of parochialism from these chapters. Is parochialism good or bad?

17. Gandalf takes his leave of the hobbits because they "are grown up now." What becomes the last step in their "growing up" process as they enter the Shire? Do you think such a step is always necessary in "growing up"? Have you had an opportunity or experience similar to this, in which you had to take charge and solve a problem?

18. A saying attributed to Edmund Burke states: "The only thing necessary for the triumph of evil is for good men to do nothing." How does this saying apply to the situation in the Shire upon the return of Frodo and his companions? One of the Chief's ruffians tells them that the Shire "wants waking up and setting to rights." How is this statement congruent with Burke's statement (though this is certainly not the intention of the ruffian)? How do the hobbits deal with the situation?

19. Describe Frodo's attitude toward the confrontation with the ruffians in the Shire. What was Merry's and Pippin's attitude toward the confrontation? How did these two attitudes complement each other? What might have happened if either one had been absent?

20. What changes do we see in Sam in these last chapters? What do they imply about his future? Use examples from the text to illustrate your answer.

21. What effect does the last paragraph of the book have on you? Do you think it is an effective ending? What do you think Tolkien was trying to communicate with the final words? How would the feeling of the end of the novel be different if Sam's words had been, "Well, they're gone"?

Dig Deeper:

22. When Barliman Butterbur learns "there is a king again," he wonders why the King should be concerned with Bree, "sitting in his big chair up in his great castle, hundreds of miles away," until Sam tells him that the new King is none other than "Strider." How might having a king who is familiar with him and his circumstances help Butterbur? How might it help Butterbur trust the king more?

Read Psalm 8:1–4 and Hebrews 4:14–16. In what way are these verses similar to Butterbur's situation? How can these verses bring comfort to us?

23. Of the new order in the Shire, Farmer Cotton tells Frodo, "It all began with Pimple . . . . Seems he wanted to own everything himself, and then order other folk about." What human tendency might Lotho's behavior illustrate? Read Matthew 6:19–21, 24, 31–33; Luke 12:13–21; 22:24–27. According to these verses, what should be our attitude toward wealth and power?

24. How does Frodo's reasoning for refusing to have Saruman slain reflect the apostle Paul's teachings in Romans 12:17–21 and 1 Thessalonians 5:15?

Why does Saruman respond to Frodo's mercy by saying "'You have grown, Halfling. . . . You are wise, and cruel. You have robbed my revenge of sweetness, and now I must go in bitterness, in debt to your mercy. I hate it and you!'"?

25. The narrator tells us that, in the years following their adventures, Sam "was pained to notice how little honour [Frodo] had in his own country," specifically

alluding to Matthew 13:54–58 and John 4:44. What function do you think these allusions serve? What might they tell us about Frodo? What might they tell us about humans in general?

26. At the beginning of Chapter 7, when Frodo feels again the pain of the Nazgûl knife in his shoulder and the memory of darkness, Gandalf says,

> "Alas! there are some wounds that cannot be wholly cured," said Gandalf.
>
> "I fear it may be so with mine," said Frodo. "There is no real going back. Though I may come to the Shire, it will not seem the same; for I shall not be the same. I am wounded with knife, sting, and tooth, and a long burden. Where shall I find rest?"

Later, when Frodo and Sam meet the elves and Bilbo as they travel to the Grey Havens, and Sam realizes Frodo intends to leave, Sam says to Frodo, "'But . . . I thought you were going to enjoy the Shire.'" Frodo responds,

> "So I thought too, once. But I have been too deeply hurt, Sam. I tried to save the Shire, and it has been saved, but not for me. It must often be so, Sam, when things are in danger: some one has to give them up, lose them, so that others may keep them."

In your own words, why can Frodo not remain in the Shire? Read Romans 8:19–23 and Philippians 1:20–25. According to these verses, how are Christians in a situation similar to Frodo's? What keeps Paul satisfied that he will remain? Do you ever feel the pain mentioned in these verses? How do you deal with it?

27. At the end, as the travellers ride to the Grey Havens, Tolkien describes them this way:

> Then Elrond and Galadriel rode on; for the Third Age was over, and the Days of the Rings were passed, and an end was come of the story and song of those times . . . . and among them, filled with a sadness that was yet blessed and without bitterness, rode Sam, and Frodo, and Bilbo, and the Elves delighted to honour them.

With all that is now finished, with all they were losing and leaving, why do you think they were able to feel "sadness that was yet blessed and without bitterness"? As you see things ending, as you move on to different places and times of your life (moving, new job, college, friends leaving, possibly a death), how will you face them? How might the following verses help you to face such situations with "sadness that was yet blessed": Romans 8:18, 28; 1 Corinthians 13:12; Philippians 3:8?

Overview Questions and Essay Topics for *The Return of the King*

Questions:

1. Tolkien wrote *The Lord of the Rings* to be read as one work, but it was the publisher's decision to divide it into three novels—a decision with which Tolkien disagreed. The result of the dividing of *The Lord of the Rings* is that the usual plot structure, or dramatic structure, applies to the *trilogy* and not necessarily to each of the three novels. However, Tolkien also composed *The Lord of the Rings* as a series of smaller "books," and though each of these is only a small part of the greater plot, each was organized with a plot formula similar to a larger work.

   Customarily, a novel can be divided into a five-part "dramatic structure," consisting of:

   1) the *exposition* or introduction, in which the writer establishes the tone and setting of the work, introduces most of the characters, and gives the audience the necessary facts and background to understand the action;

   2) the *rising action* or complication of the plot, which draws the characters into increasing conflict;

   3) the *crisis, climax,* or *turning point* of the plot, which sets in motion the eventual conclusion of the plot's central conflict;

   4) the *falling action,* in which the condition of the central character either improves or deteriorates, necessarily leading to

5) the *dénouement* (day noo MAH) or resolution, in which all plot complications are finally sorted out, and all subsidiary mysteries and misunderstandings are cleared up.

The diagram that follows represents dramatic structure. *The Return of the King,* as the third novel and Books V and VI, is primarily concerned with the climax, falling action, and dénouement of the complete story.

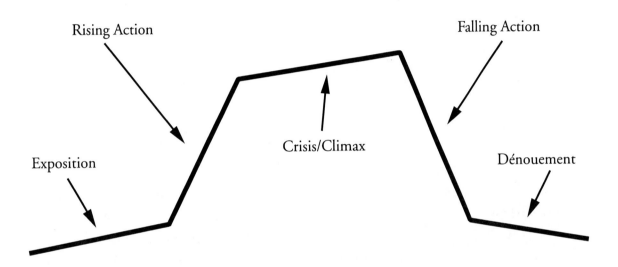

Under the headings below for the climax, falling action, and dénouement, write down the chapters (there may be one or more and the chapters may not be consecutive) in which each occurs and list at least three events from those chapters that illustrate the dramatic structure. One example is provided for you in Crisis/Climax.

Crisis/Climax:
Book V, Chapter 10: The armies of the West gather before the Black Gate and are attacked by the forces of Sauron.

Falling Action:

Dénouement:

2. In telling the story of Éowyn and Faramir's courtship, Tolkien further develops the theme of pity that runs throughout *The Lord of the Rings*. How is Faramir's pity for Éowyn different from the pity for Gollum shown by Frodo and Sam? How is it similar? What do we learn about pity by considering these examples together?

Essays:

In the following essays, be sure to state a strong thesis and support it with specific reference to the text. We suggest that the student do at least several essays, although the choice of appropriate essays and the number of essays to be done is up to the student and instructor.

1. The title *The Return of the King* perhaps carries special connotations for Christians as we await the return of Jesus Christ, who has promised to come again to rule the earth. Tolkien seems to have woven this theme into this last book of *The Lord of the Rings*. Research the scriptures commonly associated with prophecies of Christ's return—sometimes referred to as the Second Coming—and compare them with images of Aragorn and Gandalf in *The Return of the King*. (Some of these scriptures have been listed earlier in this study guide.) Discuss the parallels you find in specific images and in general patterns, and also note the differences. In the grand scheme of the book, and taking into account Tolkien's theory of "Myth," what do you think Tolkien was trying to do with these parallels?

2. Compare descriptions of Minas Tirith during Aragorn's reign with descriptions of the new Jerusalem in Revelation 21, 22:1–6. Discuss the parallels you find in specific images and in general patterns. Do you think Tolkien was consciously alluding to these scriptures? Again, taking into account Tolkien's theory of "Myth," what do you think Tolkien was trying to do with these passages?

3. As they journey toward Mount Doom, Sam remarks, "We must take [the road] and chance our luck, if there is any luck in Mordor." What instances of "luck" help Frodo and Sam make their journey through Mordor? Do you think it *is* luck that helps them? How does Gollum's presence and fate at the Cracks of Doom—his actions at the most critical moment of the Quest—shape your understanding of luck in *The Lord of the Rings*? Do you think Christians should believe in luck? Consider the following texts when developing your answer: Genesis 50:20; Esther 4:14; Ecclesiastes 9:11; John 9:1–3; Romans 8:28.

4. The theme of healing—for people, kingdoms, and lands—seems to be a major element of *The Return of the King*. What was the source of healing for people? Who could and could not be healed? Why? How were the kingdoms or land healed? Do you see ways in which you can apply the examples of healing from *The Return of the King* to your life?

5. In one of his letters, Tolkien claimed, "I do not think that even Power or Domination is the real centre of my story . . . . The real theme for me is about something much more permanent and difficult: Death and Immortality." [Tolkien, *Letters* 246] How do you see this theme developed in *The Return of the King*, both in the characters' lives and as a more global theme?

6. Compare and contrast *The Return of the King* with one or both of the following film adaptations:

   • *The Return of the King* (animated; Rankin-Bass, 1980)
   • *The Lord of the Rings: The Return of the King* (live action; New Line Cinema, 2003)

   How faithful are these adaptations to the source material? What changes do the filmmakers introduce, and, in your opinion, do these changes enhance or detract from the story and its themes?

Overview Questions and Essay Topics for *The Lord of the Rings*

The following questions may be used as subjects for essays or for discussion. In writing essays, be sure to state a strong thesis and support it with specific reference to the text. We suggest that the student do at least several essays, although the choice of appropriate essays and the number of essays to be done is up to the student and instructor.

1. Characters in a work of literature can be static or dynamic. A *static character* changes little or not at all during the course of the novel; a *dynamic character* grows and changes as the novel progresses. Sometimes the change is actual, as a character learns more and adapts, and sometimes the change is in the reader's perception as more is learned about the character. Choose one of the following dynamic characters and explain how he or she changed over the course of the trilogy: Frodo, Sam, Merry, Pippin, Éowyn, Aragorn.

2. In one of his letters, Tolkien referred to Sam Gamgee as "the chief hero" of *The Lord of the Rings* [Tolkien, Letters 161]. Do you agree with Tolkien's statement? Be sure to define "heroism" as you understand it in the work, and to articulate clearly how you think Sam either rises to or falls short of that definition. If you disagree that Sam is the chief hero, state who you believe *is* the main hero and explain why.

3. *Narcissism* is a psychological condition characterized by self-preoccupation and lack of empathy, among other traits. Research narcissism and compare your findings with Saruman's words and actions throughout *The Lord of the Rings*. Write a five- to ten-page paper detailing your findings. Be certain to support your statements with quotations from the text and properly reference outside sources.

4. Some have speculated that the One Ring is a metaphor for sin or temptation. Review the way in which the Ring interacts with Frodo, particularly in *The Fellowship of the Ring* and *The Return of the King*, and explain how it gains influence, the consequences of acting under the influence of the Ring, whether it ultimately can be resisted after its use, and the long-term effects of its influence and the wounds it causes. Compare the Ring and Frodo's struggles with these scriptures on sin and temptation: Mark 14:37, 38; Romans 7:18–25; 1 Corinthians 10:14; 1 Timothy 6:11; 2 Timothy 2:22; Hebrews 2:18–3:1, 4:14–16; 1 Peter 5:6–11.

5. From the death and resurrection of Gandalf, to the servanthood of Sam, to the triumphal entry into Minas Tirith of King Aragorn and the start of a new age, messianic images are sprinkled throughout *The Lord of the Rings*. Do a survey of *The Lord of the Rings* and catalog passages or events that carry a messianic allusion or theme. Discuss the significance of these allusions, given Tolkien's views on Myth, "subcreation," and evangelium.

6. The dénouement or resolution portion of a story is the part in which all plot complications are finally sorted out and all subsidiary mysteries and misunderstandings are cleared up. *The Lord of the Rings* has a particularly long dénouement in Book VI, Chapters 5–9, of *The Return of the King*. Review the dénouement chapters and write a paper detailing the previously unresolved elements of *The Lord of the Rings* that Tolkien clears up in these chapters. Also discuss any issues that you find are still unresolved at the end of the story.

7. Why did Tolkien title his work *The Lord of the Rings*? Why is Sauron, the book's ultimate personification of evil, its title character? Would you have given the book a different title and, if so, what would it have been? What, if anything, might we learn about the work by closely examining Tolkien's choice of title?

8. Construct a well-reasoned argument regarding the significance of interdependence in *The Lord of the Rings*. Consider the relations between the various races of Middle-earth, between its many territories and kingdoms, or between individual characters. What lessons, positive and/or negative, can readers draw from the relationships in *The Lord of the Rings*?

9. One of the titles considered by Bilbo for his and Frodo's journals was "The War of the Ring." Much of *The Lord of the Rings* concerns preparations for war and actual battle. Review the complete trilogy and put together a position paper reflecting Tolkien's attitudes toward war and its causes. You might consider the following questions: Does Tolkien believe in a just war (research the idea of "just war")? What contributes to war? Is war inevitable in international relationships? From what you read, do you believe Tolkien is a pacifist, a hawk (someone who advocates war), or something in between?

10. What is the nature of evil as it is presented in *The Lord of the Rings*? Consider such questions as: Who or what is identified as evil? Is evil always easily identifiable in Middle-earth? What factors seem to cause evil to flourish and persist? Is evil the absence of good; an active, intelligent force in and of itself; or something else? How is evil to be defeated, if it can be? How might Tolkien's view of evil seem shaped by Christian faith and the Bible? Support your conclusions with specific references to the text.

11. Critic Tom Shippey argues that Tolkien wanted his characters to demonstrate the virtue of heroism as it is presented in Old Norse mythology, with which Tolkien was intimately familiar and of which he was very fond. In Old Norse mythology, the ultimate triumph of good over evil is not assumed. Shippey states, "In a sense this Northern mythology asks more of people than Christianity does, for it offers them no heaven, no salvation, no reward for virtue except the sombre satisfaction of having done right." [Shippey 150] Explore the degree to which this understanding of heroism is present in *The Lord of the Rings*. Cite specific situations and quotations from the text to either defend or refute Shippey's contention that the Norse idea of heroism, as presented here, motivates Tolkien's characters.

    Another issue may be whether it is true that followers of Christ are virtuous primarily for the rewards of salvation and heaven or whether they are motivated by some other reason. If there is another reason, what is the Christian's motivation to be virtuous? How does the heroism present in *The Lord of the Rings* compare with the Christian motivation for virtue? Refer to Job 1, 2; Matthew 22:34–39; and Mark 12:28–34.

12. In an article in Time magazine, as director Peter Jackson's film version of *The Two Towers* was being released, critic Lev Grossman stated, "If *The Lord of the Rings* is a fantasy, it is ultimately a fantasy about growing up and putting childish things aside." [Lev Grossman, "Feeding on Fantasy," *Time,* 2 December 2002: 94] Defend or refute Grossman's claim, citing specific situations and quotations.

13. At the end of *The Hobbit,* when Bilbo Baggins observes that "the prophecies of the old songs have turned out to be true, after a fashion," Gandalf responds,

> "Surely you don't disbelieve the prophecies, because you had a hand in bringing them about yourself? You don't really suppose, do you, that all your adventures and escapes were managed by mere luck, just for your sole benefit? You are a very fine person, Mr. Baggins, and I am very fond of you, but you are only quite a little fellow in a wide world after all!"

In *The Fellowship of the Ring,* when the Ring passes to Frodo and Frodo laments that it ever found its way into his family, Gandalf tells him,

> "Behind that there was something else at work, beyond any design of the Ring-maker. I can put it no plainer than by saying that Bilbo was *meant* to find the Ring, and *not* by its maker. In which case you also were *meant* to have it. And that may be an encouraging thought."

Write a paper tracing the instances of providence (sometimes called "fate" or "luck" in the story) throughout *The Lord of the Rings.* Do you see patterns of a greater power directing events? What does this reveal of Tolkien's worldview and faith.

14. At the end of his quest, Frodo failed to destroy the Ring—when the moment of decision arrived, Frodo succumbed to the Ring's dominance and its promise of power. Several other characters in the novel, however, managed to resist its allure. Review the instances in which characters did not succumb to the temptation of the Ring and describe how they resisted. Also discuss why you think Tolkien did not have one of them carry the Ring to Mount Doom, and/or why Tolkien decided to have Frodo fail.

15. The theme of mercy or pity is woven throughout *The Lord of the Rings,* beginning in *The Fellowship of the Ring* when Frodo cries out, "What a pity that Bilbo did not stab that vile creature [Gollum], when he had a chance!" (referring to an event in *The Hobbit,* Chapter 5), and continuing to Sam deciding, as he prepared to kill Gollum on the side of Mount Doom, that though "it would be just to slay this treacherous, murderous creature, . . . there was something that restrained him: he could not strike this thing lying in the dust, . . . utterly wretched" (*The Return of the King,* Book VI, Chapter 3). Gollum, Gríma Wormtongue, and Saruman seem to receive the most pity and mercy in the story, yet none of them comes to a good end. Review the situations in which they are shown mercy. Do you think they deserved it? Should they have received it? Do their ends justify the mercy shown to them? How do the following scriptures compare with the above situations: Micah 6:8; Matthew 5:7, 7:1, 2; Luke 6:36; Colossians 3:12, 13? Should mercy be based on our expectations of others or their actions, or should it be based on something else?

16. Tolkien has come under fire from some critics for not having enough female characters in *The Lord of the Rings* or for treating his female characters as secondary and weaker characters. Review the female characters in *The Lord of the Rings.* Do you agree with the criticism that there are too few, or that they are "weaker" characters? Support your position with specific references to the text.

Project Ideas:

1. Tolkien himself wrote about "nothing beyond the first few years of the Fourth Age," although he did begin a story set a century after Aragorn's death. He did not finish it because he believed "the King's Peace would contain no tales worth recounting; and his wars would have little interest after the overthrow of Sauron. . . ." [Tolkien, *Letters* 419] Do you agree? Try writing your own "tale of the Fourth Age." You may use characters established in *The Lord of the Rings,* or you may invent your own; write your story in prose or poetic form (or, as Tolkien did, using both); illustrate your story if you wish. Along with your story, provide a one- to two-page statement outlining the choices you made in thinking about and writing your tale and how you see your tale as consistent with the framework for Middle-earth established by Tolkien himself.

2. Dramatize a key scene or scenes from *The Lord of the Rings*. Along with your dramatization, provide a one- to two-page statement explaining why you chose the scene(s) you did and what choices you, as adapter, had to make in bringing the scene(s) to life.

3. *Anthropomorphism* is the giving of human characteristics to a nonhuman object or creature. For example, in Book VI, Chapter 3, Tolkien writes, "there flowed whispering along the ground a thin cold air," giving a breeze or wind the ability to speak. Anthropomorphism gives movement and, sometimes, personality to otherwise inanimate things. Effective use of anthropomorphism can infuse a scene with greater meaning or purpose.

   Go through *The Lord of the Rings* and find examples of anthropomorphism and collect them in a notebook. Use these examples to write one or more poems, using as many of your examples of anthropomorphism as you can in each poem. The poems may be free verse, consisting primarily of connected images or perceptions, or they may be more traditional, using the images to communicate an idea or theme.

4. As Frodo prepares to leave the Shire for the Blessed Realm, he tells the grieving Sam,

   > . . . I have been too deeply hurt, Sam. I tried to save the Shire, and it has been saved, but not for me. It must often be so, Sam, when things are in danger: some one has to give them up, lose them, so that others may keep them.

   To understand what Frodo is talking about, and to discover whether this is a feeling others have in crises and life-and-death situations, interview soldiers or veterans, police officers, emergency medical technicians, and/or fire fighters. Read to them Frodo's words and ask whether they feel that the words in some way describe their feelings and experience. If possible, record your interviews on audiotape or videotape and edit the interviews into a documentary.

Related Resources

(* A study guide for this title is available from Progeny Press.)

Other Works by J. R. R. Tolkien:

The Lord of the Rings*
The Fellowship of the Ring*   series published by Ballantine Books
The Two Towers*
The Return of the King*

The Silmarillion   Ballantine Books and Houghton Mifflin Co.

The Hobbit*   Ballantine Books

Smith of Wootton Major and   Ballantine Books
   Farmer Giles of Ham

Sir Gawain and the Green Knight   Ballantine Books

Roverandom   grades 4 & up, Houghton Mifflin Co.

The Tolkien Reader   Ballantine Books

The Father Christmas Letters   Houghton Mifflin Co.

The Letters of J. R. R. Tolkien   selected and edited by Humphrey
       Carpenter with the assistance of
       Christopher Tolkien, published by
       Houghton Mifflin Co.

Books of Related Interest:

The Space Trilogy
Out of the Silent Planet*   by C. S. Lewis, grades 9 & up, series
Perelandra*   published by Simon and Schuster
That Hideous Strength

The Chronicles of Narnia

*The Lion, the Witch and the Wardrobe**	by C. S. Lewis, grades 4 & up, series published by HarperCollins
*Prince Caspian**	
The Voyage of the Dawn Treader	
The Silver Chair	
The Horse and His Boy	
*The Magician's Nephew**	
The Last Battle	

Books About J. R. R. Tolkien or *The Lord of the Rings*:

Tolkien: A Biography	by Humphrey Carpenter, Houghton Mifflin Co.
The Complete Guide to Middle-Earth: From The Hobbit *to* The Silmarillion	by Robert Foster, Ballantine Books
Christian Mythmakers	by Rolland Hein, Cornerstone Press
Tolkien: Man and Myth	by Joseph Pearce, Ignatius Press
Tolkien: A Celebration	by Joseph Pearce, Ignatius Press
Finding God in The Lord of the Rings	by Kurt Bruner & Jim Ware, Tyndale House Publishers, Inc.
The Atlas of Middle-earth	by Karen Wynn Fonstad, Mariner Books
J. R. R. Tolkien: Author of the Century	by Tom Shippey, Boston: Houghton Mifflin, 2001.

Books about C. S. Lewis:

Surprised by Joy: The Shape of My Early Life	by C. S. Lewis, Harcourt Brace

Films and Video:

The Hobbit	1977, animated, Rankin-Bass productions
The Lord of the Rings:	

The Fellowship of the Ring	2001, directed by Peter Jackson, PG-13
The Lord of the Rings:	
The Two Towers	2002, directed by Peter Jackson, PG-13
The Lord of the Rings:	
The Return of the King	2003, directed by Peter Jackson, PG-13

Answer Key

Book V, Chapters 1–3

Vocabulary:

1. a; 2. heirlooms: b, livery: a; 3. c; 4. a; 5. b; 6. b; 7. a; 8. a; 9. b; 10. c; 11. b; 12. a; 13. a; 14. b

Characterization:

dialogue: "'Denethor is . . . proud and subtle, a man of far greater lineage and power'"—proud, great, and powerful; "'But I know already sufficient of these deeds for my own counsel against the menace of the East'"—makes up his own mind and doesn't necessarily want others' input; "'Now tell me your tale, my liege,' said Denethor, half kindly, half mockingly"—proud, belittling; "'the Lord of Gondor is not to be made the tool of other men's purposes, however worthy. And to him there is no purpose higher in the world as it now stands than the good of Gondor; and the rule of Gondor, my lord, is mine and no other man's'"—proud, jealous of power and position, unbending, possessive, loyal to his own, shoulders duty; "'He is not as other men of this time, . . . He has long sight. He can perceive, if he bends his will thither, much of what is passing in the minds of men, even of those that dwell far off. It is difficult to deceive him, and dangerous to try'"—perceptive, intelligent, dangerous to cross; "'And the Lord Denethor is unlike other men: he sees far. Some say . . . he can read somewhat of the future; and that he will at times search even the mind of the Enemy, wrestling with him. And so it is that he is old, worn before his time'"—inspires awe and loyalty, wise, penetrating, diligent, perceptive, old, worn.

physical action: "a pale smile, like a gleam of cold sun on a winter's evening, passed over the old man's face"—cold, lacking love or substance; "almost as if he saw a line of smouldering fire, drawn from eye to eye, that might suddenly burst into flame"—Denethor struggles for power over Gandalf; "under the piercing eye of the Lord of Gondor, stabbed ever and anon by his shrewd questions"—sharp, almost cruel.

physical description: "his carven face with its proud bones and skin like ivory, and the long curved nose between the dark deep eyes"—hard, cold, inflexible, impenetrable; "a pale smile, like a gleam of cold sun on a winter's evening, passed over the old man's face"—cold, lacking love or substance; "Denethor looked indeed much more like a great wizard than Gandalf did, more kingly, beautiful, and powerful; and older"—stately, kingly; impressive.

physical surroundings: "No hangings nor storied webs, nor any things of woven stuff or of wood, were to be seen in that long solemn hall; but between the pillars there stood a silent company of tall images graven in cold stone," "avenue of kings long dead," "the throne was empty. At the foot of the dais, upon the lowest step which was broad and deep, there was a stone chair, black and unadorned, and on it sat an old man"—cold, hard, unadorned, empty.

Questions:

1. Although Pippin is impressed by the city's strength and beauty, the narrator reveals that "it was in truth falling year by year into decay." Pippin notices and wonders about the silent, empty houses.

2. A dead tree stands in the courtyard. It is significant because it was once the White Tree that blossomed when the realm of Gondor was at its height. The tree traces its lineage to "the Uttermost West"—the Blessed Realm—"before days when the world was young" (Book II, Chapter 2). It represents the glory of Gondor, now gone to decay.

3. Denethor first learned Boromir had died when the Anduin River carried Boromir's broken horn to Minas Tirith prior to Gandalf's and Pippin's arrival. Boromir's death has severely depressed Denethor, leading him to feelings of despair. He says the "darkness" facing Minas Tirith—the threat of Sauron's advancing armies—is "less now" to him than "[his] own darkness" of grief over his son's death.

4. Pippin offers his service to Denethor "in payment of [his] debt"—i.e., to honor the fact that Boromir sacrificed himself in trying to save Pippin and Merry from the orcs (see Book III, Chapter 1). Within himself, however, he also acknowledges that he is motivated by pride: he wants to prove to Denethor that hobbits, or "halflings" as Denethor calls them, can be of service in this time of need.

5. Gandalf and Beregond tell Pippin that Denethor "has long sight. He can perceive, if he bends his will thither, much of what is passing in the minds of men, even of those that dwell far off"; "[s]ome say . . . he can read somewhat of the future; and that he will at times search even the mind of the Enemy, wrestling with him."

6. The news from Lebennin is that a fleet manned by "the corsairs of Umbar" approaches the Anduin River, and thus threatens Minas Tirith and its allies, primarily by creating another battle front and tying up troops that could have gone to the defense of Minas Tirith.

7. Halbarad brings Aragorn a tall staff with a furled banner, or standard, made in secret by Galadriel.

8. Aragorn communicated with Sauron, who reacted to Aragorn with fear, because Aragorn—the rightful King—represents the greatest threat to Sauron's plan to dominate Middle-earth. Aragorn says he used the *palantír* because he is its "lawful master" and he wanted Sauron to see him and understand that he was a threat. Aragorn hoped the sight of him and the realization of what that meant might goad Sauron into moving before he was ready and perhaps into making a mistake.

9. "The Dead" are those who, in the time of Isildur, promised to fight against Sauron but broke their promise and refused to fight because they had once worshiped Sauron. As a result, Isildur cursed them to never lie in peace until they had fulfilled their original vow. Aragorn follows the Paths of the Dead because they offer the quickest way to Pelargir on the Anduin, which needs Aragorn's aid against the corsairs if the corsairs are to be defeated before they reach Minas Tirith.

10. A Rider who calls himself Dernhelm offers to carry Merry on his horse. Dernhelm is slighter of build than the other warriors and so adding Merry will not overburden his horse. Dernhelm recognizes Merry's great desire to go and tells him, "Such good will should not be denied."

Thinking About the Story:

11. Gandalf rebukes both Pippin and Denethor for not being aware of their position within a larger world. Pippin had never taken the time to learn about countries and peoples outside of the Shire, and so had no way to prepare himself for meeting a man such as Denethor. Denethor, though he knew much of the outside world, thought about it only in relation to its importance to Gondor. Neither Pippin nor Denethor looked at their place within a larger world. Instead they looked upon the world only through their own interests.

12. Answers will vary. Pippin offers his allegiance during a moment of feeling a sense of obligation toward Boromir and also feeling piqued at some slight in Denethor's attitude toward him and toward hobbits in general. Merry pledges himself to Théoden out of a sudden impulse of love for the old king. Both decisions are spur of the moment, have the effect of separating the hobbits from their friends, leave the hobbits wondering what they have done and whether it was wise, and tie the young hobbits to two of the most important leaders in the coming wars. The greatest difference is that Merry's pledge was motivated by love, whereas Pippin was motivated by duty. The reader may see the motivations reflected in the rulers.

13. Responses will vary, as both Aragorn and Éowyn make strong arguments throughout this passage. Aragorn concentrates on her duty to the needs of her people; Éowyn argues that she is wasted in her current capacity, and that she is left to be sacrificed when all the men are gone. In this argument, point of view seems to be everything.

14. Responses will vary. Tolkien may be reflecting that people tend to romanticize or dramatize events after they are over, forgetting the violence and sadness of events, or changing them into the way we *wish* to remember them. On the other hand, in later years the events may be distilled into potent emotional symbols and memories, without the specific pain of direct involvement. The songs may well mention the pain and sadness of the wars, much as the elvish songs often concern the pain of separation and passing, but the immediacy is gone and the events are distilled into a more bittersweet universal experience.

15. The tone of this passage and the end of the chapter becomes very lyrical and structured, using repetition and formal language. For example: "The lady Éowyn greeted them and was glad of their coming"; "And she answered as one that likes not what is said:" "Then he kissed her hand, and sprang into the saddle, and rode away, and did not look back." The passage reads like an epic poem, such as *Beowulf*, which is written for oral recitation. This may be Tolkien's way of giving Aragorn's ride on the Paths of the Dead an epic feel. However, the actual ride under the mountains changes point of view to Gimli, the character most unlike the rest of the party. Gimli is horrified and terrified by the trip, and his point of view is a strong contrast to the epic element before and after the ride in darkness—perhaps to make it more accessible to the reader or to give it a greater sense of realism. The lyrical, epic language before and after the ride under the mountains may illustrate what Tolkien earlier was saying about the songs of Rohan: it is easier to be "romantic" about an event before or after, but during the event one concentrates on dealing with the immediate experience.

Dig Deeper:

16. The modern saying is, "Where there is a will, there is a way." The modern saying means something like, "If you desire something strongly enough, you can find a way to accomplish it"; Dernhelm's saying could be paraphrased, "If you are willing, a way will present itself" or "a way will be provided." The difference is subtle, but possibly very important: the modern saying is self-based—"you can do anything, if you believe or want it badly enough," might be another paraphrase. Dernhelm's proverb implies another active force—something else "opens" a way—perhaps alluding to God's providence. As to whether these sayings are true, answers may vary; however, logically they cannot be universally true. For example, no matter how much he might will it, a man cannot bear a child, nor can a petite person be a lineman in professional football, and business success requires special circumstances beyond strong desire and willingness to work. However, nothing can be accomplished if one does not have the will to attempt it and strive for it. For discussion, see also Genesis 22:1–18; Exodus 3:1–4:20; Numbers 13, 14; 1 Chronicles 17; Romans 1:8–13.

17. Answers will vary. Merry desires to be with the king to whom he has pledged service and allegiance, yet the king has ordered him to stay behind. Éowyn suffers the same fate. However, when Merry is given the opportunity to secret himself into the king's troops, he does so almost without hesitation. His desire is to continue to serve the king in the king's presence. Whether he is right to disobey to king's direct order to remain behind is debatable, though later in the story Tolkien makes the decision seem obvious.

18. Answers will vary. Interpretations may vary, but all three scriptures show us that discernment is a matter of being aligned with God's Spirit. Discernment is presented as a gift from God. Solomon asks God for "a discerning heart" so that he may "distinguish between right and wrong" (1 Kings 3:9; the Hebrew literally reads "a hearing heart," implying that true discernment comes from an openness to God's voice). The teacher in Proverbs urges us to "lean not on your own understanding," but rather to "[t]rust in the Lord will all your heart" (Proverbs 3:5). Paul says that discernment of God's will comes only after we have submitted ourselves fully to God and God has "transformed" us: "offer your bodies [i.e., your whole selves] as living sacrifices . . ." (Romans 12:1–2). Criteria for choosing the best way among several apparently right options will vary. A hierarchical procedure for decision may follow these lines: 1) discard anything clearly forbidden in the Bible; 2) consider anything clearly recommended in the Bible; 3) prioritize based on what would be most honoring to God; 4) use the knowledge and wisdom God has given you to choose a course of action.

19. As discussed previously, the Dead are those who broke an oath to fight with Isildur against Sauron. Their situation may be considered a parallel with fallen humanity who, beginning with Adam, disobeyed God and sided with evil. As a result of this disobedience—this "oathbreaking"—"death reigned" (Romans 5:14) "for the wages of sin is death" (6:23). We, like the Oathbreakers, are trapped in death, unable to save ourselves. However, "at just the right time, when we were still powerless, Christ died for the ungodly" (5:6). Verses 5:9–11 tell us that by Christ's blood, we have been reconciled to God—the offense has been erased—and we now can rejoice in God and life. "[T]he gift of God is eternal life in Christ Jesus our Lord" (6:23b). The Paths of the Dead, the trip through the forbidden caves under the mountains, is a powerful image of death—in fact, it *has* meant death for all who attempted it before Aragorn—but Aragorn emerges alive on the other side, bringing with him not only his companions but the Oathbreakers, the Dead, and he offers them life again, or at least the chance to enter the afterlife in peace. Romans 14:9 calls Jesus Christ "the Lord of both the dead and the living;" Aragorn's title "King of the Dead" may be an allusion to this christological affirmation.

20. Answers may vary. Aragorn himself says he is tired, and it may be simply that he is more easily provoked because of exhaustion. However, it seems true that, in a sense, Gimli has forgotten to whom he is speaking. Aragorn has travelled with his companions for many miles and many days as little more than wise Strider, a Ranger from the North, vagabond protector of the free people. However, he is also Aragorn, descendent of Isildur, rightful king of Gondor, and the time is coming for this side of Aragorn to come to the fore. Gimli and his companions know this, but still tend to relate to Aragorn only as their friend. Aragorn has the right to use the Stone, and the ability to master the Stone, because he is the direct descendent of Isildur which carries the rights, responsibilities, and power of that position. Aragorn has begun to make the transition, and his companions need to be aware of it.

Book V, Chapters 4–7
Vocabulary:
1. h; 2. d; 3. e; 4. n; 5. p; 6. s; 7. i; 8. q; 9. c; 10. a; 11. j; 12. f; 13. l; 14. m; 15. r

Literary Technique: "Archaic" Language

Examples in Chapter Six include, but are not limited to: sentence structure (e.g., "Great was the clash of their meeting"), Scripture-like interjections (e.g., "But lo!", "And behold!"), vocabulary choices (e.g., "Begone"), the singular second-person form of address ("thee" and "thou"), Éomer's poetic rallying of his troops after King Théoden's death and again upon seeing the ships from Umbar, the poetry that concludes the chapter, and even the sudden switch from "Merry" to "Meriadoc" following the hobbit's stabbing of the Lord of the Nazgûl. Tolkien probably intended the "archaic" language to strike readers as exalted, as befits a lofty subject matter; namely, the War of the Ring. The language highlights the significance and drama of the events unfolding in a way in which more casual language might not. Examples of such language in the trilogy as a whole abound; Tolkien's comments above, for example, refer to Théoden's dialogue with Gandalf in Book III, Chapter 6, "The King of the Golden Hall." Accept other examples. Such language contrasts with less formal styles, such as the "rustic" style in which many hobbits speak throughout Book I, the blunt speech of Gimli, or the "broken" style in which Gollum speaks in Books IV and VI. Tolkien chose styles appropriate to the characters speaking or to the immediate subject matter.

Questions:

1. Faramir brings news of his encounter with Frodo, Sam, and Gollum, including their decision to enter Mordor by way of Cirith Ungol (see Book IV, Chapter 6). Denethor seems displeased because he understands what Frodo has and believes Faramir should have brought the Ring to him, to protect and use as a last resort. He feels certain his other son, Boromir, would have brought the Ring to him. Denethor's displeasure is ironic because—as Gandalf correctly points out—Boromir wished to take the Ring for himself (see Book II, Chapter 10). In Boromir's confrontation with Frodo, it became clear that Boromir wanted the Ring for his own use and would not have given it to his father.

2. First, Gandalf entertains, but then rejects, the idea that Pippin's use of the *palantír* may have roused Sauron. Then, he wonders if Aragorn has used the *palantír* (as we in fact know he has—see Book V, Chapter 2). Gandalf thinks that such an act is in keeping with Aragorn's character: "bold, determined, able to take his own counsel and dare great risks at need." Ultimately, however, Gandalf reserves judgment.

3. Gandalf states he fears Gollum will betray the hobbits, but also notes that "a traitor may betray himself and do good that he does not intend."

4. The chief captain of Mordor's armies—in his life before becoming a Ringwraith—was the King of Angmar, a sorcerer. Gandalf refers to the legend that the King of Angmar cannot be killed "by the hand of man." The King of Angmar is slain, not by a man, but by a woman—Éowyn, disguised as Dernhelm—with assistance from Merry, who also is no Man, but a hobbit.

5. Faramir is seriously wounded, felled by a poisoned arrow. Denethor keeps solitary vigil by his son's bed and begins to descend deep into despair. He also shows some signs of remorse for having treated Faramir harshly; e.g., "I sent my son forth, unthanked, unblessed, out into needless peril, and here he lies with poison in his veins."

6. The Woses are "the Wild Men of the Woods" who are "[r]emnants of an older time." They aid the Rohirrim by leading them to Minas Tirith by way of a long-forgotten path. Woses and the people of Gondor coexist, but not easily or peacefully; Ghân-buri-Ghân's comments indicate that the "Horse-men" (i.e., the Rohirrim) of Gondor hunt the Woses "like beasts." The Woses also feel that the people of Gondor look down on and treat them like "children," as Ghân-buri-Ghân's reaction to Éomer's condescending questioning illustrates.

7. Denethor does not know that the Rohirrim come to Minas Tirith because the errand-riders of Gondor were killed, presumably by orcs, and could not reach Denethor with the Red Arrow and the news it signified. Indeed, they were killed when they turned back towards Rohan *away* from Minas Tirith; they were not able to reach the City at all because of the siege.

8. The flaw in the Lord of the Nazgûl's plans is that the darkness cast over Gondor by the power of Mordor provides cover under which the Rohirrim may come to the aid of Minas Tirith, and the forces of Mordor left no troops dedicated to covering their flank. The few orcs that were left to the rear of Sauron's army were bent on destroying the outer fortifications and were not prepared to defend against an attack from the rear.

9. Although the men of Minas Tirith think the ships from Umbar carry "corsairs," or pirates allied with Sauron, Aragorn and his company actually sail on them.

Thinking About the Story:

10. Tolkien uses the armor—"the livery and gear of the Tower"— which Denethor gives Pippin to show a change in Pippin's awareness of himself and his situation. For example, as Pippin sits with Beregond on the Guard-towers of Minas

Tirith, the hobbit reflects that "it seemed years . . . since he had sat there before, in some half-forgotten time when he had still been a hobbit, a light-hearted wanderer touched little by the perils he had passed through. Now he was one small soldier in a city preparing for a great assault, clad in the proud but sombre manner of the Tower of Guard." The weight of the armor reflects his understanding of the "weight" of his situation: "In some other time and place Pippin might have been pleased with his new array, but he knew now that he was taking part in no play. . . ." Pippin's role has changed from a wanderer who took part in whatever adventure he stumbled into, to a participant in a formal, disciplined, and structured role. He now answers to a higher authority for his actions and cannot eat, sleep, or move without permission. Pippin's somber mood throughout this passage suggests that he is not comfortable with knowing how he has changed. Responses to the personal application question will vary.

11. The "white rider" probably is an allusion to Revelation 19:11–21, though it also may bring in the image of Revelation 6:2. The white horse and rider in Revelation 6:2 is an image of a conqueror, which is not quite the actions of Gandalf in this instance. The image in Revelation 19 is of the warrior-messiah-king Jesus Christ, returning to bring ultimate victory to earth. Students' discussion of the impact of this image on the passage will vary, but it carries with it the image of great power, ultimate good, and an unstoppable force. Of course Tolkien appears to be presenting Gandalf as a "savior figure" in limited ways; Gandalf's function at this point seems to be to bring hope and temporary deliverance, not to effect ultimate deliverance for Gondor, since the war against Mordor continues. In contrast, when the glorified Christ appears in Revelation 19, God's war against God's enemies is finished in a decisive way.

12. Responses may vary; accept reasoned interpretations supported by specific reference to the text. Denethor and Faramir's relationship as father and son is, at the least, strained. The formal way in which the two relate to each other— e.g., "May I have your leave, father?"—reflects this conflict. Apparently, Denethor always valued Boromir over Faramir, as his expectations that Boromir would have brought the Ring to Gondor indicate. Faramir feels compelled, in fact, to remind his father, "I too loved" Boromir. Thus, Boromir's death complicates Faramir and Denethor's relationship: Faramir mourns the loss of a brother, while Denethor mourns the loss of a son whom he considered a "better" son than Faramir. In fact, Denethor tells Faramir that he wishes Faramir had died instead of Boromir ("'. . . Boromir is gone.' 'Do you wish, then,' said Faramir, 'that our places had been exchanged?' 'Yes, I wish that indeed,' said Denethor."). Faramir apparently feels the need to earn his father's respect and love, as his willingness to defend the River and the Pelennor "in [Boromir's] stead" shows. Yet, through it all, Gandalf affirms to Faramir, "Your father loves you . . . and will remember it ere the end." Students' personal connection to the issue of difficult parent-child relationships will vary, and responses should be treated with sensitivity and respect.

13. Aragorn can use a *palantír* without danger because, as noted previously, he is its "lawful master," though even he admits that he had barely enough strength to do so (Book V, Chapter 2). Denethor, in contrast, shows no such self-knowledge. Gandalf says that Denethor no longer knew "the limits of his own strength." The contrast between Aragorn and Denethor could teach us that we must know our own strengths and weaknesses in order to remain free; Sauron used Denethor's lack of self-knowledge to gain influence over him and Minas Tirith. Accept other reasonable responses.

14. This passage repeats the word *and,* creating run-on sentences and other grammatical errors. In one case, Tolkien even begins a sentence with *and.* Technically, this passage would be considered an offense against grammatical writing, but it creates a sense of movement that fits with the picture of waves of Rohirrim riding across the plain, fighting and flowing over the enemy. Read aloud, the passage gives the sense of a series of waves of action, topped or connected with *and.* Therefore, viewed grammatically the passage is "bad" writing, but it communicates the author's intent and creates a palpable sense of the scene. By the latter standard the passage is "good" writing.

Dig Deeper:

15. As do the people of Minas Tirith, the people of Jerusalem admire their city's defenses: its "towers," "ramparts," and "citadels." Yet Psalm 48 does not place ultimate confidence in these structures, but in the God to whom they bear witness. As Professor Jon Levenson notes, "Vv. 13–15 call upon the congregation to conduct a visual inspection of Mount Zion and its fortifications in order to learn the lesson that YHWH is Israel's God and leader forever . . . . The very sight of [the Temple city complex] yields knowledge of God, without the utterance of a word." [Jon D. Levenson, *Sinai and Zion: An Entry Into the Jewish Bible* (San Francisco: Harper San Francisco, 1985) 146–147.] In contrast, the people of Minas Tirith seem to trust in their city's defenses in and of themselves and so are terrified when the forces of Mordor break through them. Psalm 46, which also includes language about a strong city (vv. 4–5), explicitly teaches that because *God* is in the city's midst, it shall not be moved.

16. Dread and despair are terrible because, as Denethor illustrates, they either paralyze us into inaction or lead us, by our actions, to defeat ourselves before our enemies do. Denethor abandons his role as a Steward, forsakes his own people as their defender, risks the life of his son and loses his own life on a funeral pyre—all because he has given up hope. During Ben-hadad's siege of Samaria, the king of Samaria and his captain give in to despair as Denethor does (e.g., 2 Kings 6:33; 7:2), even though Elisha promises deliverance from God (2 Kings 7:1), as Gandalf urges Denethor to hold out hope: "There is much yet that you can do." Because he despaired, the king of Samaria's captain, like Denethor, does not live to see his city's deliverance (2 Kings 7:20). Accept other reasonable, informative parallels. Rather than despair, Elisha trusts God to solve the situation in 2 Kings, and Gandalf, Pippin, and Beregond believe that as long as they are alive they can still choose the course of their own actions. The lepers in 2 Kings have a similar, though more fatalistic attitude: though they expected to die, they chose to act in a manner that held out the greatest hope, and in so doing they discovered God's defeat of Ben-hadad's army.

17. As a consequence of his despair, Denethor abandons his role as a Steward, forsakes his own people as their defender, tries to take the life of his son, and loses his own life on a funeral pyre. His people are left leaderless and Gandalf has to step in to assume the leadership role, limiting his effectiveness and taking him away from his own duties. As a result, people die whom Gandalf may have saved, and in the end, Gandalf is pulled from the battlefield to save Faramir's life. Christian thought often considers despair a sin because despair does not allow room for the action of God, with whom all things are possible (compare Genesis 18:14; Matthew 16:26 and parallels; Luke 1:37). The alternative to despair is trust in God, as Psalm 130 urges Israel to do. In John 16:33, Jesus presents himself as the alternative to despair because he has overcome the world of opposition to God and God's people. In 2 Corinthians 4, Paul testifies that his knowledge of God through Christ (v. 6) keeps him from despair, even in the most difficult of times (vv. 8–12; compare 12:10). Personal answers will vary.

18. Like the Lady Éowyn, Beregond faces a choice between conflicting duties and responsibilities: Denethor's orders to stay at his post, and what Pippin argues is a higher duty to help save Faramir's life by finding Gandalf, whom he hopes will put a stop to Denethor's despondent, suicidal behavior. Like Jesus in Matthew 12, Pippin argues that human life is a higher priority than any "orders" (as these Pharisees perceived their interpretation of the Law to be). Jesus shows that working for the good of human life actually fulfills the Law (compare Matthew 5:17), since the Law was given for humanity's good.

19. Denethor's statement reveals the flaw of overwhelming, unhealthy pride, manifested in his sinful plan of suicide (let alone his intention to end Faramir's life along with his own) and his desire to control his own fate. The biblical texts teach that God opposes the proud (e.g., Proverbs 8:13; Isaiah. 2:11, 17) and exalts the humble (e.g., Luke 1:51), and that such pride leads to destruction (e.g., Proverbs 16:18). In contrast to being like Denethor and insisting on ruling to our own end, Jesus instructs us to pray that God's kingdom will come and that God's will alone will be done (Matthew 6:10; Luke 11:2).

20. Denethor was deceived because, while looking in the *palantír*, "he saw . . . only those things which [Sauron] permitted him to see." In other words, Sauron did not want his foes to see the whole truth about their situation. Almost any group or individual trying to convince someone to adopt their position uses this ploy, consciously or unconsciously, to some extent. Examples will vary, but may include such things as information from political parties or other special interest groups, product advertising, etc. Having incomplete knowledge traps us and can lead, in extreme cases, as it does in Denethor's case, to despair and death. In contrast, when we follow Jesus Christ, he frees us not only by revealing truth to us (John 8:32) but by being Truth itself (John 14:6), though this does not mean Christians automatically see the truth in all situations. We can pray for clear vision of our true situation from God. We must also get information from many sources to compare facts and opinions.

21. Beregond sees the greater picture than just Gondor's situation. He sees Gondor as a critical part of the battle against evil, but not the only hope: "we are but one piece in it, whatever pride may say." He also, with Pippin's help, sees life beyond the war, even after defeat: "There are still other fastnesses, and secret ways of escape into the mountains. Hope and memory shall live still in some hidden valley where the grass is green." His perspective is not limited to only what befalls Gondor, nor is it just limited to this particular horrible time. Denethor sees little of importance outside of Gondor, he and Gondor are all that is important: "'the Lord of Gondor is not to be made the tool of other men's purposes, however worthy. And to him there is no purpose higher in the world as it now stands than the good of Gondor'"; "'And where will other men look for help, if Gondor falls?'" Other examples may be given. Clearly Beregond was more clear of heart and mind and persevered under the strain. Knowing he was part of a greater plan, he did not carry the

weight of the world upon his shoulders, nor did he despair when defeat appeared certain. He knew there were other men and other nations who would carry on. Denethor believed Gondor bore the fate of the Western peoples and that his leadership was necessary to Gondor. He could not see the greater picture, and so when he expected defeat, he saw the overthrow of all and did not wish to continue.

In 1 Kings 19, Elijah is under attack from the queen once again, and believes he is alone in fighting for God: "I am the only one left, and now they are trying to kill me too." Believing he is alone in fighting evil, he despairs. First, God gives Elijah several things to do, then God informs him that he is not alone, "Yet I reserve 7,000 in Israel." In a sense, God tells Elijah to take his eyes off himself and get to work, and then he will see all the others still loyal to God. Denethor's situation is very similar; he has taken his eyes off all others, even going so far as to despise them and belittle them, and he views himself as the lone power for good. However, he does not listen to Gandalf's admonitions as Elijah listens to God's instructions.

22. Answers and examples may vary. A case may be made for hubris, hamartia, and a combination of the two. Denethor certainly suffers from hubris, even at the end. Specific examples will vary; accept reasonable responses. Denethor repeatedly tells Gandalf that he knows more than Gandalf and sees what others cannot. He believes himself able to withstand the power of the Ring and use it against Sauron: "'If I had this thing now in the deep vaults of this citadel, we should not then shake with dread under this gloom, fearing the worst, and our counsels would be undisturbed. If you do not trust me to endure the test, you do not know me yet.'" He believes that only Gondor can stand against Sauron, that Gondor is the last hope of the good: "'And where will other men look for help, if Gondor falls?'" He believes that only he and his family can rule Gondor, and without him the kingdom will descend into barbarism: "'Nay, nay, whatever may now betide in war, my line too is ending, even the House of the Stewards has failed. Mean folk shall rule the last remnant of the Kings of Men, lurking in the hills until all are hounded out.'" As for hamartia, the most convincing argument may be made for Denethor's use of the *palantír*, although you could also make a case for his apparent disdain for and mistreatment of Faramir. The hamartia may have occurred because of pride in his own powers or wisdom, or ignorance of the power of Sauron or the full workings of the stone. Other positions may be taken and should be judged by evidence provided from the text.

Book V, Chapters 8–10
Vocabulary:

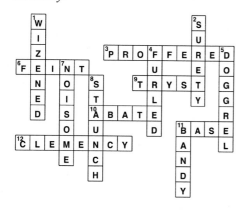

Questions:

1. Since Merry stabbed the Lord of the Nazgûl, he is unable to use his right arm, which feels cold. These are symptoms of a malady the leeches of Gondor call "the Black Shadow," which leads to death.

2. Ioreth remembers an old saying: "The hands of the king are the hands of a healer."

3. *Athelas* is the plant Aragorn uses in healing Faramir, Éowyn, and Merry. Also called *kingsfoil*, it is significant for its healing properties; in fact, it is "a healing plant that the Men of the West brought to Middle-earth" (Book I, Chapter 12). Ioreth says *athelas* is unremarkable in appearance—"if I were a king, I would have plants more bright"—yet its aroma when crushed is sweet and "wholesome." We first learned of *athelas* in Book I, Chapter 12, when Aragorn used it at Weathertop in bathing Frodo's shoulder, which had been wounded by the Lord of the Nazgûl's Morgul-knife.

4. Gandalf tells Éomer that Éowyn's malady truly began while she served the failing Théoden as Wormtongue poisoned his mind and spirit with false words: "'Think you that Wormtongue had poison only for Théoden 's ears?'" Constrained by caring for Théoden in that poisonous atmosphere, unable to share her brother's "deeds of arms" in the "free fields," Gandalf says Éowyn felt more useless than the staff on which Théoden leaned.

5. The people of Minas Tirith call Aragorn "Elfstone," referring to the green stone he wears as a pendant, given to him by Galadriel. It is also the name "foretold at his birth that he should bear," "chosen for him by his own people."

6. Gandalf advises an attack against Sauron because such an attack will draw Sauron's attention away from Frodo, giving him a last chance to destroy the Ring.

7. If the Ring is destroyed, according to Gandalf, all of Sauron's strength and works of destruction will be destroyed because they rest on the foundation of the Ring's power. "[H]e will lose the best part of the strength that was native to him in his beginning" because he placed that power in the Ring. (Chapter 9).

8. Aragorn says Pippin "has yet to match" Merry's deed of helping slay the Lord of the Nazgûl. He puts Pippin's presence at the final battle against Sauron in perspective by telling Merry that "in truth all are now in like danger," and that Merry may yet have to face "a last stand."

9. Imrahil urges the heralds to announce "The King Elessar is come!" rather than "The Lords of Gondor are come," because, even though Aragorn has not yet reclaimed his ancestral throne, his right to rule is not in dispute, and the royal title will cause Sauron more concern ("it will give the Enemy more thought"). Sauron knows of Aragorn since Aragorn used the *palantír*, and the knowledge made him insecure. He also may believe that Aragorn has the Ring and is trying to secure his hold on power. The return of the King of Gondor is more likely to concern Sauron than an attack by the Lords of Gondor, who have remained in static power for many years.

10. Pippin slays the chief of the hill-trolls, who is about to kill Beregond.

Thinking About the Story:

11. Responses may vary, but both Gandalf and Aragorn seem to regard Ioreth as the wiser of the two, because she remembers the prophecy of the true king's healing hands and fit it to the correct circumstances. She not only remembered old sayings, she had the sense to apply them at the right time, even though she did not recognize or understand the full impact or exact application of the words, and she knew where it could be found. The herb-master, for all his knowledge of herbs' and plants' many names, and even the old sayings, dismisses the old sayings as "rhymes of old days which women such as our good Ioreth still repeat without understanding." Students will draw various conclusions. One possible response is that when the time comes to act, practical knowledge is more important than academic knowledge, and there are times when we must trust our own intuition or less "acceptable" sources of information, such as folklore and legend. Indeed, legends and folklore often grow from a seed of truth. Note that Gandalf and Aragorn lose patience with the herb master primarily because he does not act and because he looks down on the other forms of knowledge; his mind is closed to other options.

12. Responses will vary. Merry seems to mean that we should be content with our situation in life. Students may react to this statement positively or negatively. You may wish to point out that Merry does not say people should never aspire to other situations, but that it is best "*first*" (emphasis added) to appreciate one's life as it is.

13. Gandalf uses an extended agricultural metaphor comparing the war against Sauron to the task of farming: "*uprooting* the evil in the *fields* that we know, so that those who live after may have *clean earth to till*. What *weather* they shall have is not ours to rule." His point is that the defenders of Minas Tirith have a responsibility to do what they can against evil now; such action is the best service they can render to those who come later. Whether or not other, presently unknown evils will threaten people in the future is not the responsibility of the present. Personal reactions and applications will vary. Some may read Gandalf's judgment as pessimistic: as if to say, "There will always be evil in the world, and we can't change that fact." Others may take that same reading as a realistic description of life. Still others will react—as Tolkien seems to have intended (see further Gandalf's words, "[B]etter so [to act now] than to perish nonetheless . . . and know as we die that no new age shall be.")—to Gandalf's words as a positive statement of personal responsibility for action when presented with the chance to act. Compare with Gandalf's comments to Frodo in Book I, Chapter 2: "All we have to decide is what to do with the time that is given us."

14. The "Mouth of Sauron"—that is, Sauron's emissary or spokesperson at the Black Gate—was the Lieutenant of the Tower of Barad-dûr, but the narrator tells us that his name is known neither to history nor, any longer, to himself. Students' interpretations of this fact may vary; one reasonable conclusion—accept others that students can support—is that Tolkien here portrays that evil robs us of our individuality, our personality, our identity. Students could cite several

other illustrations of this view from the trilogy as a whole; perhaps the most dramatic are the Ringwraiths, who were once mortal men, but who now "exist" only—and quite literally—as shadows of their former selves, having no personal identity. Gandalf says they are "shadows under [Sauron's] great Shadow, his most terrible servants" (Book I, Chapter 2.) Even the Lord of the Nazgûl has a crown but not a head ("A crown of steel he bore, but between rim and robe naught was there to see"—Book V, Chapter 6), indicating the paradox that his existence is only that of "nothingness." (For further elaboration of this concept, consult Tom Shippey, *J. R. R. Tolkien: Author of the Century*, pp. 128–135.)

15. The Mouth of Sauron produces Sam's sword, a grey cloak with an elven-brooch, and Frodo's *mithril*-mail coat. He says these tokens are "'marks of a conspiracy'" between the races of the West, says "'he who bore these things'" might be "'one dear to you,'" and warns that "'Sauron does not love spies, and what his fate shall be depends now on your choice.'" The Mouth of Sauron is implying that they have caught a spy that was sent with the cooperation of all the races of the West. The reader can conclude from his statements that he has not captured Sam and Frodo (the Mouth refers only to "he" and "the creature"), he does not know their mission (he believes the "creature" was a spy), Sauron does not yet have the Ring (there would be no need for this dramatic charade and he would know the mission was not to spy). Therefore, there is still hope that at least one of the two hobbits is still free and still trying to take the Ring to Mount Doom.

16. Pippin is horrified when he hears Gandalf reject the terms given by the Mouth of Sauron, apparently condemning Frodo to a long, painful death in Mordor. He suddenly feels as if it were best "to die soon and leave the bitter story of his life, since all was in ruin." He also wishes that Merry were with him so they "might die together." He both understands Denethor's desire to get his death over quickly, and his desire to die with his son. However, Pippin also decides "now I must do my best," and he draws his sword to fight. Pippin does not give up on ultimate hope. He believes the end has come, but he still sees his duty.

Dig Deeper:

17. Among the images and language the narrator uses to describe the effects of *athelas*: morning dew; fresh, clean air from snowy mountains or a far-off sea; "the scent of orchards, and of heather in the sunshine full of bees." The language and images are united by their creation of an impression of, as Ioreth says, "wholeness," of refreshment, of renewal. The imagery in the biblical texts describe God's loving forgiveness of sin (Hosea 14), knowledge of God through Christ, which is life itself (2 Corinthians 2), and Christ's life of love for us which he calls us to emulate (Ephesians 5). Like Tolkien's language, these biblical texts use aromatic images (dew; fragrance; etc.) to describe renewal, refreshment, and "wholeness." Students will draw various connections; accept well-reasoned answers. Perhaps Tolkien, a devout Christian, drew either consciously or subconsciously on the biblical tradition of sweet-smelling images to evoke a sense of newness; on the other hand, Tolkien insisted his work was not allegorical, and such images would evoke that sense virtually universally, and the Bible's use of such images gives them content specific to God's actions towards us, most particularly in Jesus Christ.

18. Psalm 23 sings of God guiding and comforting us "through the valley of the shadow of death" (23:4; note NIV marginal note, "darkest valley") as a shepherd guides his sheep. Jesus speaks of himself as the Good Shepherd in John 10, whose voice the sheep recognize and follow when he calls. Aragorn's healings of Faramir, Éowyn, and Merry can thus reflect the far greater "healing" that God in Jesus Christ performs by calling sinners from death to abundant and everlasting life.

19. Aragorn is presented as a Christ-like healer, most especially, perhaps, in his healing of Éowyn. As Jesus heals Jairus' daughter when all hope for her life seems gone, so does Aragorn heal Éowyn when, in her sword-arm, "there now seems no life." As Jesus orders the little girl, "*Talitha koum!*," so does Aragorn order both Éomer and Éowyn, "[A]wake!" In the Matthew passages, Jesus heals many in the crowds who gather around him, and it is recognized as a fulfillment of prophecy. Aragorn also fulfills prophecy as he goes out and heals the wounded after the battle. Neither Jesus nor Aragorn reserve their healing to the important or most "worthy," they healed freely. Ephesians 5:14 also pictures Jesus' act of salvation as a call to awaken from the dead.

20. Answers will vary. Aragorn is telling Pippin that Merry will be saddened by his experience, but it will not cause him depression or to be morose. Merry will learn from his experience; perhaps it will put life into clearer perspective, help him to value the time and friendships he has, cause him to take greater joy in the moment or greater responsibility for others' needs. In 2 Corinthians 7, Paul acknowledges that a previous letter to the believers in Corinth "caused [them] sorrow" (7:8), yet Paul does not regret that sorrow, because it produced in the Corinthian Christians greater "earnestness" and "eagerness" to obey God's will for them, "to see justice done" (7:11) in their dealing with a congregational conflict (consult biblical commentaries as needed and appropriate). Paul teaches, "Godly sorrow brings repentance that leads

to salvation and leaves no regret, but worldly sorrow brings death" (7:10). Paul acknowledges that the people of Corinth used their sorrow and pain to change their behavior and become better people.

21. Responses will vary. Some may say that if an action does not achieve its end, in this case victory over Sauron, it is wasted. Others may say that an action is great or right in and of itself, whether others approve or praise it or not. The Matthew passage says we are not to base our actions on the approval of men, but to act for the approval of God. The other verses instruct us to act in the strength and for the glory of God. If everything we do, we do for God's approval and glory, then our actions will be great and praiseworthy whether others recognize them or not.

22. Answers may vary. Aragorn acts with great humility after the battle for Minas Tirith. Though he is the rightful king, he refuses to claim his title until the rulers of the city are prepared to formally bestow the title upon him. He even refuses to camp within the city to avoid the appearance of occupying it as its ruler or intimidating the people of the city. After he heals the wounded, he quietly leaves and returns to his own tent. In fact, after the battle, he suggests that they all submit to Gandalf's leadership. Note that Aragorn's actions and humility lead the Prince to declare that he will follow him wherever he leads. As Jesus says in Matthew and Luke, Aragorn acts much more like a servant than a lord. He works long into the night healing common soldiers, then quietly leaves to rest. He does not demand recognition of his rightful title but instead waits until the proper people are willing to ask him to assume his title. Aragorn does not demand and force, he serves and asks.

Book VI, Chapters 1–4

Vocabulary:

1. *welter:* correct; turmoil; a rolling and surging
2. *irrevocable:* correct; impossible to retract or revoke
3. *aghast:* incorrect; shock, horror, amazement
4. *bemused:* incorrect; bewildered, confused, deep in thought; *din:* correct; loud, jumbled noise
5. *bastion:* correct; considered secure, as a defensive stronghold
6. *stinted:* correct; give limited amount, restrict, give sparingly
7. *vassals:* incorrect; feudal servant, landholder owing allegiance to feudal lord; *foundered:* correct; to sink, collapse
8. *insatiable:* incorrect; impossible to be satisfied
9. *beleaguered:* correct; surrounded, harassed
10. *lay:* incorrect; (as used in the book) a ballad, song, narrative poem
11. *esquire:* correct; candidate for knighthood, a knight's attendant
12. *serried:* incorrect; crowded closely together,

Narrative Technique: Interlacing

Reactions will vary. Interlacing can create tension and suspense in a narrative, since it allows readers to share the characters' lack of knowledge about crucial information. On the other hand, it can create tension because the reader knows things the characters do not, and so the reader can see the greater context of the characters' actions. It also helps the reader anchor the current action in the events about which she has already read. This technique may also intrude on the current action or make it difficult to keep track of all the strands of the plot. Accept other reasonable interpretations of Tolkien's use of this device.

Alliteration and Assonance:

Alliteration is underlined, assonance is in brackets.

> [A]ll was [o]minously quiet. The light was no more than that of dusk at a dark day's end. The vast vapours that arouse in Mordor and went streaming west ward passed l[o]w [o]verhead, a great welter of cl[ou]d and smoke n[ow] lit again beneath with a sullen glow of red.

Questions:

1. Sam makes his way past the Two Watchers by revealing the light from the phial of Galadriel, which causes the Watchers to fear. He and Frodo escape them when leaving Cirith Ungol by again using the phial, and also by calling on Elbereth in Elvish. The wall on which the Watchers are seated crumbles. The Watchers cry out, and, from above, a Nazgûl answers.

2. Although Frodo is at first glad and relieved that Sam has the Ring, he quickly becomes angry and suspicious of Sam's motives for wanting to help him bear it, calling him a "thief." He suddenly, and briefly, sees Sam as "a foul little creature with greedy eyes and slobbering mouth," a description that not only is reminiscent of Gollum but also mirrors the way

Frodo briefly saw Bilbo in Book II, Chapter 1, when Bilbo wanted the Ring: "a little wrinkled creature with a hungry face and groping hands." Answers will vary about the implications. Clearly the Ring has a hold on Frodo strong enough to distort his perception of his friends when they may come between him and the Ring.

3. Shagrat gets away with a bundle containing Frodo's mithril shirt, his elven cloak, and Sam's dagger. These are the trophies the Mouth of Sauron displays to Gandalf and his friends before the gates of Mordor.

4. Frodo and Sam see "dim light leak[ing] into Mordor" and hear a cry from a Nazgûl that "no longer held any terror for them: it was a cry of woe and dismay." We know these things signify the defeat of the Lord of the Nazgûl on the Pelennor Fields and the death of King Théoden.

5. Technically, they are detected, when an orc slave-driver sees them and mistakes them for small orcs because they are dressed in orc clothing from Cirith Ungol. He forces them to join the troops marching toward battle, and they eventually escape when two groups of orcs collide and intermingle at a crossroads.

6. Sam is unable to kill Gollum because he feels pity for him, having carried the Ring himself for a short time and being able to understand, if even in a limited way, the pain and torture it causes for Gollum.

7. After Frodo puts on the Ring at the Cracks of Doom, Gollum attacks the invisible Frodo and tries to wrestle the Ring from him. Unable take it, he finally bites off the finger on which Frodo wears the Ring and falls with it into the fire.

8. Gwaihir and the Eagles bear Gandalf to Mount Doom to retrieve Frodo and Sam. They are eventually taken to Ithilien to recover with the army that assaulted Mordor.

Thinking About the Story:

9. a. Genesis 37:28, 36; 45:4–7: Similar to the way Joseph was sold into slavery and carried into Egypt, Frodo and Sam are picked up by slave-drivers and taken deeper into Mordor. Both events seemed like defeats, but both turned out to be for the good.

9. b. Genesis 37:31–35: Just as Joseph's brothers took his cloak, bloodied it, and took it to their father to make him believe that Joseph was dead, Shagrat took Frodo's Mithril shirt and elven cloak and it was used by Sauron to try to convince Gandalf and his friends that Frodo was captured and beyond hope. Also, in both cases the person feared to be dead ultimately is the salvation of all the others.

9. c. Matthew 4:1–10 [Luke 4:1–13]: Just as Jesus suffers greatly and then is tempted to great power, Sam also is tempted with great power in a time of weakness and loss. Note particularly Sam's parallel with the third temptation of Christ, and that both reject the offer of power.

10. Underlined words should be "trees lurked and clung," "grass-tussocks fought," "mosses crawled," "writhing, tangled brambles sprawled." Answers about the tone may vary. The tone of the passage is bleak, grotesque, twisted. Tolkien uses the anthropomorphic words to make the plants appear more animated and horrible, as if the plants were human or animals. All of the verbs (lurked, clung, fought, crawled, writhing, sprawled) have negative connotations, as if there was evil intent or pain.

11. Answers may vary, accept reasonable examples. The biggest irony, of course, is that Gollum, not Frodo, actually accomplishes the destruction of the Ring. It is ironic that Frodo, after all the hardships and struggle to arrive at the Cracks of Doom to destroy the Ring, at the end refuses to do so. It is ironic that Gollum, fighting to get the Ring back and keep Frodo from either having or destroying the Ring, ultimately causes its destruction. It is ironic that Gollum saves not only Frodo and Sam from the horrors that would have descended upon them, but also all of Middle-earth, even though he would happily have caused them all to suffer. It is ironic that Gollum says earlier, "[W]hen Precious goes we'll die," and then fulfills his statement by causing that very event.

12. Answers about foreshadowing will vary. Solid arguments may be made for both positions. The statements do foreshadow the final events, but their importance becomes clear primarily in hindsight, whereas foreshadowing as a literary technique usually more directly and obviously points the reader in the direction the author intends to go. Foreshadowing usually is used to create anticipation in the reader, and the argument can be made that these statements are too dispersed throughout the work to create such anticipation. Instead the pattern becomes clear afterward, like one reaching the top of a hill and, from that vantage point, being able to look back and see clearly how one reached one's final position. Answers about whether Gollum's end was an ironic accident, a natural result of circumstances, or the direct result of an command or curse by Frodo will vary. Accept reasonable and well-thought-out answers.

13. The scene in Book VI, Chapter 4, in which Sam awakens in Ithilien, meets the criteria of eucatastrophe in several ways. His reaction to seeing Gandalf again is "between bewilderment and great joy," and he is moved to ask, "Is everything sad going to come untrue?" Gandalf laughs in response, "like water in a parched land"—an image of reversal, of

© 2003 Progeny Press

"sudden joyous 'turn.'" Similarly, Sam's tears turn to laughter. The answer to Sam's question, "What's happened to the world?" is, "A great Shadow has departed;" and thus the scene serves the consoling function of fairy-story as Tolkien describes it. Yet Frodo, though mostly healthy and sound, will still bear the wound of his missing finger; one could argue that this acknowledgment of Frodo's wound represents the "evidence" of defeat and failure of which Tolkien speaks—had Frodo not failed, he would not be "Frodo the nine-fingered"—yet it is not "universal final defeat," as Frodo himself had feared while on Mount Doom. Accept other reasonable responses.

14. This section is primarily presented from Sam's point of view. This may seem a little odd; one might expect to read from the main protagonist's point of view or from a more third-person point of view. Answers about Tolkien's reason for adopting Sam's point of view will vary. Considering the circumstances, Frodo's point of view might be too introspective—Sam's character is more concerned with the necessities of the journey and so is more observant of his surroundings. Accept all reasonable answers.

Dig Deeper:

15. Possible responses include: Sam's temptation is to claim the power of the Ring for himself and transform nature—turning the vale of Gorgoroth into an Edenic garden. Though Jesus is not tempted to a perfectly parallel deed (unless you count transforming nature to fulfill his own desires by turning stones to bread), yet both are tempted to work miracles through the assumption of power for their own desires. Sam's temptation does not last as long as Jesus' temptations and is therefore not as serious in nature—Sam seems almost to "shake off" the brief temptation, as opposed to Jesus' serious struggle (Matthew 4:11, where angels attend to Jesus after his trials). The two temptations suggest that power is to be used to serve others and in the manner and for the purpose proscribed. Sam resists his temptation, in part, because of his love for and desire to serve Frodo, and Jesus refuses because of his love for and desire to serve God (Matthew 4:10; Luke 4:8). Sam knows he is not meant to command "the hands of others;" similarly, Jesus resists the temptation to serve only himself, since "the Son of Man did not come to be served, but to serve, and to give his life as a ransom for many" (Matthew 20:28; compare Mark 10:45).

16. Sam sees "a white star twinkle for a while." The beautiful star causes him to reflect that "in the end the Shadow was only a small and passing thing: there was light and high beauty for ever beyond its reach." Sam is pulled out of his circumstances and becomes aware of the vastness of creation and time and realizes his—and Sauron's—small part it. In essence, Sam took comfort in the fact that Sauron is as finite as he is. Answers may vary. Just as the star represents, for Sam, "light and high beauty for ever beyond [Sauron's] reach," John 1:5 proclaims, "The light"—that is, the life brought into being through Jesus Christ, the Word of God—"shines in the darkness, but the darkness has not understood it" ("has not overcome"—NIV alternate translation). Not only did God make the earth and heavens, creations that seem permanent to us, but to him they are as transient as worn clothing. Only God has been and always will be. But in his greatness, he will still reach down to "revive the spirit of the lowly and to revive the heart of the contrite" (Isaiah 57:15), and, in Jesus, he tells us to "take heart! I have overcome the world" (John 16:33). As Sam looks up at the star shining unreachable beyond the clouds of Sauron and takes heart from its purity and permanence, we can look up to Christ who has overcome evil and promises us his peace.

17. Answers will vary, but should highlight *lembas'* ability to strengthen, in a supernatural way ("beyond the measure of mortal kind") weary travelers (an ability seen at other points in the trilogy; e.g., Book III, Chapter 3). Here we learn that, in addition, *lembas* is more potent to the degree that those who eat it rely on it alone. Without the "virtue" inherent in the *lembas,* we are told, Frodo and Sam "would long ago have lain down to die." Considering that Tolkien was a devout Christian, it is probable that *lembas* represents Holy Communion; since Tolkien was a Roman Catholic and a firm believer in the Roman Catholic Church's doctrine of transubstantiation—that is, that the elements of bread and wine in Communion literally become the body and blood of Jesus—it is likely that lembas' ability to strengthen the weary supernaturally reflects the strength given to the faithful in Jesus' body and blood. Tolkien wrote, "The only cure for sagging or fainting faith is Communion." [Tolkien, *Letters* 338] This comment would seem to suggest that Tolkien—who, to this author's knowledge, never explicitly affirmed an equivalency between *lembas* and Communion—would at least not object to his readers drawing parallels, since *lembas* aids the "fainting faith" of Frodo and Sam. John 6 records Jesus' discourse in which he calls himself "the bread of life" (6:48), "food that endures to eternal life" (6:27). *Lembas* allows those who eat it to endure physically; Jesus allows those who feed on him—figuratively by faith, as many Protestants have traditionally interpreted this text; literally, by faithful reception of Communion, as Catholics and other Christians believe—to endure to something greater, "eternal life." Those who eat *lembas* will still one day die; those who feed on Jesus will never die (6:50). In 1 Corinthians 10, Paul reminds his readers that the bread they break and eat is "a

participation in the body of Christ" (10:16); therefore, Christians "cannot have a part in both the Lord's table and the table of demons" (10:21)—a pure reliance on God that Tolkien perhaps intended to reflect in his comment that *lembas'* efficacy depends upon eating it unmingled with other food. Students may make other comparisons and contrasts, especially depending upon their faith tradition's understanding of Communion. Accept reasonable responses, and encourage discussion among the students of similarities and differences in their views on and practices of Communion.

18. Interpretations of Tolkien's comment may vary. For his part, Tolkien meant that, being a mortal who had been bearing the Ring for so long, and the corrupting influence of the Ring having been established from the beginning of the story (compare Bilbo's refusal to part with the Ring in Book 1, Chapter 1)—indeed, having been hinted at even in *The Hobbit,* in Bilbo's failure to tell Gandalf the true outcome of his riddle contest with Gollum (Chapter 6; compare *The Lord of the Rings* Prologue, Section 4; also Book I, Chapter 2)—it was not possible for Frodo to part with the Ring willingly. Frodo was not a "bad" hobbit; rather, he was, as Tolkien says in the above comment, an "incarnate creature," subject to the "temptation" and "evil" of which the Lord's Prayer speaks ("lead us not into temptation, but deliver us from evil"). Tolkien interpreted this petition of the Lord's Prayer to mean, "There exists the possibility of being placed in positions beyond one's power," [Tolkien, *Letters* 252] and we must rely on a power greater than ourselves. This is also reflected in the Romans passage: Paul clearly states that "what I want to do I do not do, but what I hate I do." Tolkien thus insisted that evil is overcome only by grace: the "mercy" and "pity" which Bilbo, Frodo, and Sam had each shown in letting Gollum live, a reflection of the ultimate grace of God. (For the foundation of this interpretation, see especially letters 181 and 191 in *The Letters of J. R. R. Tolkien,* and Tom Shippey's book, *J. R. R. Tolkien: Author of the Century.*) When Paul asks who can rescue him from this body of death, he answers himself: Jesus Christ! (Romans 7:25)

Book VI, Chapters 5–6
Vocabulary:
1. gainsaid: spoken against; 2. puissant: potent; 3. renown: fame; 4. palfrey: a riding horse, as opposed to a war horse; 5. niggard: stingy

Questions:
1. Éowyn still feels "unhealed" because she is not playing a part in the final battle against Sauron; also, her thoughts are with Aragorn, whom she believes she loves. The Warden pronounces her fully healed only after she and Faramir are betrothed to each other, suggesting that their love has healed her.

2. Aragorn tells Faramir that he and his heirs will fill the office of Steward for as long as Aragorn and his descendants remain on the throne.

3. Aragorn wants Frodo and Gandalf to crown him, because he knows that he has received his inheritance as King "[b]y the labour and valour of many" others than himself.

4. Aragorn treats Beregond with both mercy and judgment. Beregond's actions during the crisis over Denethor are punishable by death, yet Aragorn exiles Beregond instead because he acted out of love for Faramir, and Beregond will serve as captain of Faramir's guard in Ithilien.

5. Aragorn wants the members of the Fellowship to be present at his wedding to Arwen.

6. Gandalf charges Aragorn to order the beginning of the Fourth Age of Middle-earth, the Age of Men, for "[t]he Third Age of the world is ended." He also tells Aragorn that he and other Men must bear the burden of fighting evil.

7. Aragorn sees a sapling of the Eldest of Trees. It is significant because it is planted in place of the withered tree in Minas Tirith. It is a symbol of a new beginning. When it blossoms in June, it is the sign that Aragorn's wedding to Arwen draws near.

8. Just as Lúthien chose mortality in order to be with Beren, so has Arwen chosen mortality in order to be with Aragorn. Because she will die, she cannot go to the Grey Havens—place of the immortal elves—with her immortal father, Elrond. If he wishes, Frodo may travel to the Havens with Elrond instead of Arwen.

9. Arwen gives Frodo a white gem on a silver chain, to bring him aid when troubled by his memories of the fear and darkness of his Quest.

10. The engagement ("trothplighting") of Faramir and Éowyn.

11. Éowyn gives to Merry a horn, a family heirloom. Anyone who sounds the horn in time of need will be guaranteed the aid of friends and will strike fear into the hearts of foes.

12. According to Gandalf, Saruman was able to persuade even Treebeard to let him go free. He presumably did this by exploiting Treebeard's dislike for "the caging of live things."

13. Saruman warns that they will find the Shire "less good . . . than [they] would like."

Thinking About the Story:

14. When the Ring is destroyed and Sauron is defeated, the people of Minas Tirith experience the "sudden joyous turn" characteristic of *eucatastrophe*. While Faramir's thoughts are of Númenor—a land that fell into utter darkness—he does not believe Gondor shall suffer the same fate: "a hope and joy are come to me that no reason can deny." Likewise, the people of the City sing "for the joy that welled up in their hearts from what source they could not tell." The joy cannot be explained, but can surely be experienced. Yet Lady Éowyn's continued sadness—"it seemed that in all the City she only was ailing and sorrowful"—also marks the event as eucatastrophic, for it does not—using Sam's words to Gandalf in the previous chapter—make "everything sad . . . untrue." Even so, Faramir is right to believe that—in an ultimate sense—no "darkness will endure." The defeat of Sauron, the greatest evil threatening Middle-earth, is a promissory pledge of the defeat of other real but lesser evils. Accept other reasonable responses, supported by reference to the text.

15. Personal opinions will vary.

16. The exchanges between Ioreth and her kinswoman appear unexpectedly in the high pomp and circumstance of Aragorn's entrance into the city, and Ioreth's quaint, slightly misinformed statements introduce humor into an otherwise stately passage. Answers will vary about Tolkien's intent in putting Ioreth into this scene; accept reasonable answers. The inclusion of Ioreth's homey statements remind the reader that not all of the participants in or observers of this pageant are quite as impressed or stately as the direct participants. Though everyone is glad of the return of the king, not everyone is as aware of or concerned with exactly how it all takes place. The common person is more concerned with the practical effects on her own life. This will be seen again later as the hobbits return to Bree and the Shire.

17. Responses will vary. Some possible motives behind Saruman's spurning of Gandalf's and the hobbits' offer of help are: anger ("All my hopes are ruined, but I would not share yours"); resentment ("Will you still order my goings, and are you not content with my ruin?"); humiliation ("I do not doubt that [Galadriel] has brought you this way to have the pleasure of gloating over my poverty"); accept other reasonable responses. From the specific example of Saruman, we may generalize that hubris causes us to reject what would be most beneficial to us, or that clinging to our self-pride at all costs ultimately leads to ruin (compare Gandalf's comment: "[O]nce more you are going the wrong way"); accept other reasonable conclusions. Answers to the personal application questions will vary. Saruman probably cannot believe in their kindness and mercy because he cannot imagine them giving it without ulterior motives. It implies that Saruman has very little kindness or mercy within him.

18. Responses will vary. Perhaps—as is often the case, for example, in abusive relationships—the "comfort" of a known quantity, even if it be an abusive person, is preferable to the unknown of starting a new life on one's own. The fear of a totally different situation can be terrifying—what if things get worse? Students may or may not find Wormtongue sympathetic. Granted, it does not seem to have been Tolkien's intent to present him sympathetically, but reflection on Wormtongue as "[a]lways beaten and cursed" may lead to a more nuanced view of Wormtongue and his situation. He is one of the story's villains, to be sure, and it cannot be denied that he has made wrong choices and will do so again. However, even those who rightly suffer the consequences of wrong choices can be pitied—as, for example, we have seen various characters pitying Gollum throughout the narrative. Accept reasonable responses, and respect differences of opinion. Be especially sensitive to students who have experienced the damaging effects of abusive relationships in their lives or in the lives of their friends and loved ones.

19. This scene of Gandalf and the elves described as "grey figures, carved in stone, memorials of forgotten things now lost in unpeopled lands" is reminiscent of or parallel to the carved figures of the Púkel-men in the Dunharrow, "carved in the likeness of men." Answers may vary. The implication seems to be that Gandalf and the elves are ending their time of influence in the world, and eventually they will become lost in time like the Púkel-men, "memorials of forgotten things."

Dig Deeper:

20. Answers will vary. Both suicide and choosing to be allowed to die from injury or illness involve choice, and so in that way are similar. On the other hand, suicide creates death where otherwise there would be none, whereas choosing not to treat injuries or illness allows things to take their natural course to death. Circumstances vary so much that what may appear wrong in one instance may appear right in another. For instance is it wrong to not stop loss of blood in an accidental amputation? Is it right to not resuscitate a terminally ill patient whose heart has stopped? Accept thoughtful, well-reasoned answers, and perhaps use this question as a class discussion. Answers about Éowyn's statement if she could have seen the future may vary, but it is hard to imagine her choosing death if she knew that Sauron would be defeated, the king would return victorious, and she would find love.

21. Responses will vary. Students should note similar calls to rejoice (e.g., Psalm 98:6, though this is a call to rejoice in the divine king, not a human monarch); promises of security (e.g., Psalm 48:1–3, the city blessed by God the "Great King"); royal victories over enemies (compare Psalm 2:4–6, in which God "scoffs" at his foes because he has established the Messiah on Mount Zion); and eternal blessing (e.g., Psalm 23:6, which Tolkien may explicitly echo by saying Aragorn the King "shall dwell among you/ *all the days of your life*" [emphasis added]). Unlike the Eagle's song, however, the psalms, as already noted, praise God as Sovereign and not a human ruler (although some psalms do praise the human king, whom ancient Israel sometimes referred to as "God's son" [e.g., Psalm 2:7]). Accept other reasonable examples of comparison and contrast, as well as reasonable responses to Tolkien's authorial intent. Perhaps, steeped in Scripture and his faith, Tolkien thought the language of the psalter a fitting vehicle for celebrating Sauron's downfall at the hands of the forces of good. Certainly his choice of psalm-like language alerts readers to the echo of *evangelium* which Tolkien believed all good "fairy-story" contains; that is, King Aragorn, with all his valor and goodness, is a "type" or reflection of King Jesus.

22. In a draft of one of his letters, Tolkien specified that Faramir's function as continuing steward was to be "representative of the King during his absence abroad, or sickness, or between his death and the accession of his heir." [Tolkien, *Letters* 324] Beyond these practical reasons, however—which students may or may not deduce—Aragorn may be correcting Faramir's misperception that, simply because Aragorn reigns as King, Faramir's work is now complete. For many generations, the Steward of Minas Tirith has acted as its ruler instead of as the representative of the king. With the return of the king, the role of steward does not end, but returns to its true function—carrying out the will of the king. Translating this supposition into Christian terms, we might say that even though King Jesus rules, we, as his subjects, are still called to be his stewards. The relationship between Aragorn and Faramir may parallel the biblical passages which clearly state that we have important responsibilities to perform on Christ's behalf: "to do good works, which God prepared in advance for us to do" (Ephesians 2:10). Those good works, which are described in greater detail throughout scripture, are to be done in obedience to God so that "men may see your good deeds and praise your Father in heaven" (Matthew 5:16). Faramir's job is similar—he will now carry out the orders of Aragorn in such a way as to bring honor to the king.

23. Answers may vary. The Daniel passage refers to God—the Ancient of Days—sitting on his throne in glory and judgment. The Revelation passages concern Jesus Christ in his resurrected glory at the end of the ages. Both passages refer to the end of time when Christ shall reign over creation in glory and all things shall be remade as God intended. The most direct allusion is to the phrase "ancient of days," referring to God sitting on his throne. Aragorn is crowned with the White Crown, Christ and the Ancient of Days have head and hair "white like wool." In general, the phrasing and rhythms are similar between Tolkien's words and the scriptures. Tolkien clearly is not equating Aragorn with God or Christ—he is mortal and has weaknesses and doubts. He seems to be using biblical language to communicate to the reader a sense of power and worthiness in Aragorn and dawn of a new age of glory and justice.

24. While students' reactions to the mercy extended to Saruman may vary, the New Testament stresses—not only in these verses, but in others like them—that because God showed us unconditional mercy by giving us Jesus Christ (Romans 5:6–8), we are called and expected to show unconditional mercy to others (Luke 6:36; Colossians 3:13). The love of God, which Christians are called to demonstrate in their relationships with others, "keeps no record of wrongs" (1 Corinthians 13:5) and "does not delight in evil" (13:6). On the other hand, Jesus wants his followers to realize that there will always be "Sarumans" in the world who reject pity, mercy, and kindness; in that case, "shake the dust off your feet" (Matthew 10:14) and move on to offer peace to others who may accept it. Rejection of the peace and mercy Christians offer does not negate their responsibility to offer it, nor does it justify anger at the rejection.

25. Examples of the theme of "passing," ending, or transitioning in these chapters include: Faramir's conviction, expressed to Éowyn, that "we stand at the end of days" (compare the apocalyptic imagery of Book VI, Chapter 3); the gradual but final dissolution of the Fellowship of the Ring; the ending of the power of the Three Rings; Arwen's choice of mortality; Gandalf's solemn charge to Aragorn, "it is your task to order [the new age's] beginning and to preserve what may be preserved," and his prediction that "the kingdoms of Men shall outlast" the Ents; the image of Gandalf and the elves in conversation appearing as "grey figures, carved in stone, memorials of forgotten things now lost in unpeopled lands" (compare the figures of the Púkel-men in the Dunharrow [Book V, Chapter 3]); Bilbo's failing memory, lack of further writing, and his song near the close of Chapter 6. Interpretations of this theme may vary; for his part, Tolkien once said the work "is really about Death and the desire for deathlessness." [Tolkien, *Letters* 262] Given his comment, the attention to the theme of "passing" may emphasize that deathlessness is impossible in this world. In fact, much of

Tolkien's mythology of the Second Age of Middle-earth implies that the great error of the Elves was to cling too tightly to this world: "The chief power (of all the rings [made by the Elves, save for the One Ring Sauron made in secret]) alike was the prevention or slowing of *decay* (*i.e.,* 'change' viewed as a regrettable thing), the preservation of what is desired or loved, or its semblance. . . ." [Tolkien, *Letters* 152] The personal answers will vary, as will interpretations of this theme with scripture. Possible connections include: Genesis 3:19 teaches that we are dust "and to dust [we] will return"—mortality is a fact of our fallen human existence. In the face of our mortality, we should pray that God would teach us "to number our days aright" and give us "a heart of wisdom" (Psalm 90:12)—i.e., that God would teach us how to use the time given to us as wisely as possible and for God's glory as much as possible. The Teacher in Ecclesiastes 3 reminds us that there is a time for all things to come and go; 12:1–7 urges us to honor God early in and then throughout our life, to "remember" our Creator "before . . . the dust returns to the ground it came from, and the spirit returns to God who gave it." Living this mortal life in proper relationship to God is a matter of urgency. Ultimately, we are promised that, through Jesus Christ, God will overcome "[t]he last enemy," death (1 Corinthians 15:26), a promise prophesied by Isaiah (25:6–8). In the end, "the perishable must clothe itself with the imperishable, and the mortal with immortality" (1 Corinthians 15:53). In 1 Corinthians 7, the issue of "passing" becomes even more pressing in the light of Jesus Christ's promised return. "Passing" is now no longer the natural progression towards decay, but a "time limit" placed upon the world by the expectation of Jesus' return. Like Tolkien's characters, then, we can—and, biblically speaking, must—live with the awareness that we are "passing," while not forgetting that the passing of "this world in its present form" (1 Corinthians 7:31) is not a cause for grief, since it will result in the full realization of the victory that God has given in Jesus Christ (compare 1 Corinthians 15:57). Similarly, Gandalf, Elrond, and Galadriel seem to view the end of their age with some sadness, but predominantly with a sense of completion of a job well done and a knowledge that things will continue, though they will be different.

Book VI, Chapters 7–9

Vocabulary:

1. insolent; ruffian; 2. uncanny; 3. abashed; 4. daunt

Questions:

1. Examples students may cite may include: Butterbur's initial, suspicious assumptions about whom has returned to the inn; Bob's new practice of going home at nightfall; the relative emptiness of the inn's Common Room; the shortage of pipe-weed.

2. Possible descriptive responses include: fearful, suspicious, violent, insulated; accept similar responses.

3. Gandalf will not accompany the hobbits to the Shire because he plans to visit Tom Bombadil and he says the hobbits are quite able to handle their problems themselves.

4. The Chief is Lotho Baggins, a relative of Frodo (see Book I, Chapter 1; Appendix C, "Baggins of Hobbiton"). He is responsible for enforcing, through his band of ruffians, a strict, legalistic, oppressive way of life in the Shire.

5. Hobbiton has been forcefully industrialized. Trees have been torn down and replaced with factory smokestacks. The hobbits have been subjected to numerous and oppressive rules.

6. Farmer Cotton says that life in the Shire began to change when Lotho "wanted to own everything himself, and then order other folk about."

7. Merry raises the Shire's defense by sounding the horn given to him by Éowyn.

8. "Sharkey" is Saruman.

9. Frodo says, "It is useless to meet revenge with revenge; it will heal nothing." He also hopes that Saruman may one day find the cure for his evil.

10. According to Saruman, Wormtongue stabbed Lotho while Lotho was sleeping; Wormtongue claims that Saruman forced him to commit the murder. Wormtongue slits Saruman's throat after Saruman insults him and kicks him in the face. Hobbit archers shoot Wormtongue immediately after Wormtongue kills Saruman.

11. Sam plants saplings to replace the many trees destroyed during Saruman's hold over the Shire and, from the box of dust given him by Galadriel, Sam drops a grain of dust in each hole with the sapling. When he is finished planting, he throws the remaining dust into the wind in the middle of the Shire. The silver nut in the box—the seed of an elvish *mallorn* tree—he uses as a replacement sapling for the Party Tree, under which Bilbo gave his Farewell Speech.

12. Generally, Frodo's illnesses confirm Gandalf's statement in Chapter 7 that "some wounds . . . cannot be wholly cured"; more specifically, Frodo falls ill on the anniversaries of his wounding at Weathertop (October 6) and his wounding by Shelob (March 13). March 25 is the anniversary of the destruction of the Ring, and the beginning of the New

Year in Gondor, and thus a date appropriate for new life and new beginnings (see Appendix B, "The Great Years"). On that date the New Age began, and a new generation is born.

13. Bilbo, Frodo, Gandalf, and the Elves depart out of Middle-earth from the Grey Havens to the "Blessed Realm" in the West, a realm set aside for the immortal elves.

Thinking About the Story:

14. Answer will vary. Some possibilities are: the hobbits' warlike attire and their obliviousness to the impression it gives those around them; the people of Bree previously not liking the Rangers and now wishing they were back; Butterbur's shock that Aragorn/Strider is King; the Bree hobbits wanting to "give a bit of interest" to Frodo's book by talking about Bree instead of just the "less important affairs 'away south'"; the gatekeeper at the Brandywine bridge telling the travellers to read the sign in the dark; the shirrifs' arresting Frodo and his companions to take them where they want to go in the first place, and then getting left behind; the ruffian's statement, "'This country wants waking up and setting to rights,'" which is exactly what the travellers intend to do, but in a manner far different from the ruffian's meaning; Rosie telling Sam, "'Well, be off with you! If you've been looking after Mr. Frodo all this while, what d'you want to leave him for as soon as things look dangerous?'"; the Cottons asking "a few polite questions" but being "far more concerned with events in the Shire"; the Gaffer complaining that while Frodo and Sam have been "'trapesing in foreign parts'" they've "'ruined my taters!'"; Saruman believing that "Sharkey" may be a term of affection, while the reader knows from a textual footnote that the term probably is irreverent or insulting; Saruman believing that Frodo and his companions were castoff "tools" of Gandalf. Instances of more traditional irony include: Sharkey being Saruman; Wormtongue killing Saruman; the last confrontation with, and death of, one of the principals of the war taking place in the Shire at Bag End; the fact that Frodo, who sacrificed so much and worked so hard to save the Shire and Middle-earth, cannot stay there any longer and must go.

15. This statement is ironic because it perfectly describes Saruman and his actions toward Wormtongue. Saruman uses Wormtongue—he seems to have no affection for him. Saruman calls for Wormtongue to follow him, though he berates him and even beats him. When the hobbits wonder about Lotho's fate, Saruman, with evident pleasure, pins the blame for his death on Wormtongue. The irony is that though Gandalf is very different from Saruman's depiction of him, Saruman has described himself.

16. Examples of parochialism will vary. Some possibilities are: the Bree hobbits wanting to "give a bit of interest" to Frodo's book by talking about Bree instead of just the "less important affairs 'away south'"; the Cottons asking "a few polite questions" but being "far more concerned with events in the Shire"; the Gaffer complaining that Frodo should never have sold Bag End and left, and while he and Sam have been "'trapesing in foreign parts'" they've "'ruined my taters!'" In a broader sense, Saruman's belief that much of what Frodo and his companions did was to get back at him, or somehow involved him, was parochial in the sense that he could think only in terms of himself (though this is more rightly *narcissism*). Also, Sam's lament that the destruction of Bagshot Row and defilement of Bag End "'is worse than Mordor! . . . because it is home, and you remember it before it was all ruined.'" As to whether parochialism is good or bad, answers will vary. It is natural and to a degree right that a person's primary concern should be with his own experiences, region, and friends and family, but if that is all he is concerned with, or if he lets his private or "parochial" welfare predominate over the general welfare, he may be in error. The parochialism in these chapters show that, on the one hand, the people of Bree and the Shire do not fully appreciate the magnitude of the world-changing events with which Frodo and his friends have been involved. However—and this caveat is important—the people who remained at home have been preoccupied with a real and pressing local crisis, the activities of "Sharkey" and his followers. The story perhaps suggests that, at times, a more limited view of one's place in the world is altogether appropriate: Bree and the Shire are, in fact, in peril, and that peril must be addressed. Note, however, that it has *not* been addressed until Merry takes action—and his perspective of his place in the world *has* been broadened!

17. The last step of growth for the hobbits is taking responsibility for their own fate and destiny—taking control of the Shire away from the ruffians and setting things right. Responses may vary about whether such a step is necessary in one's growth, although it seems apparent that it is. We may learn the right things to do, but only when we actually use the things we've learned and applied them on our own can we determine whether we have mastered them—whether we have "grown up." Answers to personal question will vary.

18. Though it can be argued that a few good hobbits did try to do something about Lotho and the ruffians, too many did nothing and the ruffians (evil) gained the upper hand and were able to dominate the Shire. The ruffian's statement that the Shire "wants waking up" is an accurate, though ironic, reflection of the state of affairs after too long with good

hobbits doing nothing and allowing a gradual encroachment of evil. The hobbits, under the leadership of Merry and Pippin, finally take up arms against the rule of the ruffians and return to a benevolent and just self-governance.

19. Frodo's position was one of mercy, nearing pacifism—he did not want them to fight unless necessary and he wanted no one killed unless it was unavoidable. Merry and Pippin had a much more militaristic, confrontational attitude. They reminded Frodo that ruffians had started the killing and that it would be nearly impossible to resist them without some killing, because the ruffians themselves had no such qualms. Together, in cooperation, these two attitudes seemed to create an effective and merciful set of actions. Under Merry's and Pippin's direction, a solid and effective defense was established that matched the ruffians' violence with coordinated attacks. Frodo made certain that the ruffians got fair notice and that those who surrendered were not mistreated. Without Merry's and Pippin's knowledge of and willingness to wage war, the hobbits might not have freed themselves from the ruffians' oppression, but without Frodo's mercy, more deaths, perhaps even atrocities, might have occurred.

20. Answers may vary. Throughout *The Lord of the Rings,* Sam has been Frodo's servant, friend, and helper. In these last chapters, however, we begin to see him emerge as his own person, important in his own right and doing work unrelated to Frodo. He goes to the Cottons' to check on Rosie, and he begins to give her more of his attention. He spends a large amount of his time travelling about the Shire caring for the planting and helping set things right. When Frodo asks him when he is going to move back to Bag End, Sam is uncertain whether he should, because he wishes to marry Rosie. When Frodo asks Sam to accompany him on his last travels, Sam makes clear that he cannot be gone long because he now has a family. Frodo later prophesies for Sam a large family, renown, and growing influence on his community. Sam's last words of the novel imply that he is set to begin.

21. Answers will vary; accept reasonable responses. The ending also serves as a beginning—Sam is back and ready to start on the next phase of his life and the new age for Middle-earth. The deep breath can be seen as a cleansing breath, as one takes when one steps outside, or as one takes as one prepares to start something new. No longer is he Frodo's helper, he is now an important person in his own right. Tolkien may have been trying to bring feelings of hope and anticipation to the end. If Sam had said, "Well, they're gone," there might have been a greater feeling of "ending" and emptiness and less of a feeling of "continuing" and growth.

Dig Deeper:

22. Because the king knows Butterbur and his circumstances, Butterbur can expect the king to know and understand his needs; they will not be an abstraction for the king. He also knows that the king will know and understand Butterbur the man, not just Butterbur, a faceless subject. Knowing these things should give Butterbur greater trust for Aragorn the King. He will know that Aragorn understands his situation and he can be assured that Aragorn will act with full understanding and with his best interests in mind. Just as Butterbur wonders why the king "in his big chair" should be concerned with him, the psalmist in Psalm 8 asks why the majestic Lord of all the earth should care for human beings. The writer of Hebrews answers: Because he has been one of us, though without sin. Just as Aragorn once walked as a commoner among the people of Bree, Jesus Christ once walked as a humble man on earth. He "has gone through the heavens," yet he can "sympathize with our weaknesses." He knows what we face because he has faced it also. Answers concerning how this can bring comfort to us may vary, but the writer of Hebrews says we can "approach the throne of grace with confidence, so that we may receive mercy and find grace to help us in our time of need." Christ knows us and is willing to give us what we need, and we can approach him humbly but with confidence.

23. Lotho's behavior illustrates the human tendency to fall prey to the temptations of wealth and power. It also illustrates the old adage, "Power corrupts." The passages in Matthew tell us to work for and gather what is eternal, not what can pass away. When God demands the life of the rich man in Jesus' parable, none of his riches can save him, nor will they benefit him anymore (Luke 12:13–21). Jesus teaches his disciples that true greatness is not in "lording it over" others as do the "kings of the Gentiles" (Luke 22:25)—and as Lotho and his ruffians began "lording it around and taking what they wanted"—but rather in serving others.

24. Frodo insists that meeting "revenge with revenge . . . will heal nothing." Paul teaches us that revenge is God's business alone (Romans 12:19); our task is to "overcome evil with good" (12:21) and to "always try to be kind to each other and to everyone else" (1 Thessalonians 5:15). Answers about Saruman may vary, but note that Romans 12:20 says that being kind and merciful to an enemy "will heap burning coals on his head." By not responding in anger or revenge, Frodo robbed Saruman of the ability to consider himself superior to Frodo—Frodo has not succumbed to either bitterness or hate as Saruman has.

25. Responses will vary. The allusions clearly connect Frodo's circumstances with Christ's in some way. Perhaps they serve to illustrate the human tendency to want to hear more about "successes" than "failures," even though, were it not for Frodo's failure at the Cracks of Doom, the Ring would not have been destroyed. From Aesop's fable, "The Fox and the Lion," we also have the adage: "Familiarity breeds contempt." Though contempt may be too strong a word in these cases, both in Jesus' case and Frodo's case the people know them so well that they find it hard to connect this familiar person with great things, particularly if he is not being "flashy" about it. In Frodo's case, he did not continue wearing fine or warlike clothing, and he had far fewer tales of exciting battles to tell than did Merry and Pippin. Frodo did not pursue attention, and so the people gradually gave him less attention and honor than Sam recognized was his due.

26. Answers will vary; accept reasonable paraphrases. Frodo says in both quotations that he has been too deeply hurt to remain in the Shire—he has changed too much to find relief and peace there anymore. The wounds he has suffered, primarily the ones in which he was deeply touched by evil, have affected him too strongly to be able to enjoy his old home. He feels he must go on to the Blessed Realm to find peace. The Romans passage discusses the bondage and pain suffered by all creation as a consequence of sin, and that Christians also suffer from the knowledge that we are not pure and free as we are supposed to be and someday will be. In the Philippians passage Paul expresses his desire to be released from this life so he can go and join Christ, but he accepts that he still has work to do. The Christian's situation is similar to Frodo's in that we recognize the evil that is in the world and within us (see Romans 7) and it gives us great pain. We long to be out of this world and with Christ, but like Paul, we recognize that God still has work for us to do; and, also like Paul, we can take great joy in what God has provided for us to do (Ephesians 2:10). Personal answers will vary.

27. Answers will vary. The elves and the hobbits recognize the fulfillment of what was needed. They had done what needed to be done and completed their tasks. There seemed to be a "rightness" to the end of what they had known, and something new was growing, and they themselves were moving on to new things. Personal answers will vary. The verses speak of looking forward to new things, when all will be clearer and glory will be revealed. In the meantime, everything is in God's hands and he works "for the good of those who love him."

Overview Questions and Essay Topics for **The Return of the King**
Questions:

1. Answers may vary. *Crisis/Climax*—Book VI, Chapter 3: Sam and Frodo trying to climb the mountain; Gollum attacking Sam and Frodo on the trail; Frodo's refusal to cast away the Ring; Gollum attacking Frodo at the Crack of Doom; Gollum biting the Ring off Frodo; Gollum falling to his death and the destruction of the Ring; Sam and Frodo getting out of the mountain and lying down, apparently to die (this and following may also be considered falling action). Book VI, Chapter 4: the arrival of the eagles, the defeat of Sauron's forces, the fall of Sauron. *Falling Action*—Book VI, Chapter 4: rescue and recovery of Sam and Frodo; reuniting of hobbit friends and the Fellowship; rest and recovery of all concerned. *Dénouement*—Book VI, Chapter 5, friendship, recovery, and betrothal of Faramir and Éowyn; crowning of Aragorn; retaining Faramir as steward; banishment and praise of Beregond; finding, planting, and blossoming of the Tree; marriage of Aragorn and Arwen. Book VI, Chapter 6: breaking up and returning to Rohan, Lorien, and Rivendell; funeral of Théoden; visit to Isengard and Treebeard; encounter with Saruman on the road. Book VI, Chapter 7: rest at Bree. Book VI, Chapter 8 & 9: the cleansing of the Shire; the journey to the Grey Havens and beyond. Note that the cleansing of the Shire has its own dramatic structure: Exposition—Frodo and his friends learn what has been happening; Rising Action—they get arrested, go to Hobbiton, rouse the Shire, have a skirmish; Crisis/Climax—the final battle with the ruffians; Falling Action—the final encounter with Saruman; Dénouement—tearing down the things the ruffians built, replanting, narration of the following years. Many other things could be added to this list—accept similar responses.

2. Accept reasonable responses. Faramir pities Éowyn because of her continuing sorrow even after she has been physically healed. He does not pity her because he finds her wretched and miserable—as Frodo and Sam pity Gollum, to one degree or another—but because he sees how her grief prevents her from knowing the joy she might know, given her health, his own love for her, and the defeat of Sauron. Yet—just as Frodo and Sam see Gollum for the hobbit-like creature he once was, Sméagol—Faramir, too, pities Éowyn because he sees her unfulfilled potential. Further, in both cases, pity does not result in the fulfillment of this potential: no matter how often he is shown pity, Gollum still betrays Frodo in the end at the Cracks of Doom; Éowyn's joy is given birth ultimately not by pity, but by love. Thus, we may learn—along with Faramir himself—that pity, while admirable because it creates empathy and solidarity, is not the same as nor is as life-transforming as love. This position is but one possible interpretation.